NAHUM
and
HABAKKUK

J. Vernon McGee

THOMAS NELSON PUBLISHERS

Nashville • Atlanta • London • Vancouver

Published in Nashville, Tennessee, by Thomas Nelson, Inc.

Scripture quotations are from the KING JAMES VERSION of the Bible.

Library of Congress Cataloging-in-Publication Data

McGee, J. Vernon (John Vernon), 1904–1988
    [Thru the Bible with J. Vernon McGee]
    Thru the Bible commentary series / J. Vernon McGee.
        p.   cm.
    Reprint. Originally published: Thru the Bible with J. Vernon McGee. 1975.
    Includes bibliographical references.
    ISBN 0-7852-1033-4 (TR)
    ISBN 0-7852-1093-8 (NRM)
    1. Bible—Commentaries.   I. Title.
BS491.2.M37   1991
220.7′7—dc20   90–41340
                                                        CIP

PRINTED IN MEXICO

6 7 8 9 10 - 05 04 03 02

CONTENTS

NAHUM

HABAKKUK

PREFACE

The radio broadcasts of the Thru the Bible Radio five-year program were transcribed, edited, and published first in single-volume paperbacks to accommodate the radio audience.

There has been a minimal amount of further editing for this publication. Therefore, these messages are not the word-for-word recording of the taped messages which went out over the air. The changes were necessary to accommodate a reading audience rather than a listening audience.

These are popular messages, prepared originally for a radio audience. They should not be considered a commentary on the entire Bible in any sense of that term. These messages are devoid of any attempt to present a theological or technical commentary on the Bible. Behind these messages is a great deal of research and study in order to interpret the Bible from a popular rather than from a scholarly (and too-often boring) viewpoint.

We have definitely and deliberately attempted "to put the cookies on the bottom shelf so that the kiddies could get them."

The fact that these messages have been translated into many languages for radio broadcasting and have been received with enthusiasm reveals the need for a simple teaching of the whole Bible for the masses of the world.

I am indebted to many people and to many sources for bringing this volume into existence. I should express my especial thanks to my secretary, Gertrude Cutler, who supervised the editorial work; to Dr. Elliott R. Cole, my associate, who handled all the detailed work with the publishers; and finally, to my wife Ruth for tenaciously encouraging me from the beginning to put my notes and messages into printed form.

Solomon wrote, ". . . of making many books there is no end; and much study is a weariness of the flesh" (Eccl. 12:12). On a sea of books that flood the marketplace, we launch this series of THRU THE BIBLE with the hope that it might draw many to the one Book, *The Bible.*

J. VERNON MCGEE

NAHUM

The Book of
NAHUM

INTRODUCTION

As I come to each new book and chapter of the Bible, some folk kid me that I always say it is the *greatest* book or chapter. Very candidly, I must say that the little Book of Nahum is not the *greatest* in the Bible, but it is a great book, and it is in the Word of God for a very definite purpose. I dare say that very few people have ever heard a sermon from the little Book of Nahum. This book has received some attention from those who speak "the wild utterances of prophecy mongers," as Sir Robert Anderson calls them. These sensationalists would have us believe that Nahum prophesied of the automobile when in the second chapter he says that "The chariots shall rage in the streets" (Nah. 2:4). That, of course, has no reference at all to the automobile, as we will see when we come to it.

What we do have in the Book of Nahum is a remarkable prophecy, but one which seems very much out-of-date. To begin with, we know very little about Nahum personally, and he has just one theme: the judgment of Nineveh, the capital of the Assyrian Empire. This is all his prophecy is about, and it has already been fulfilled; so how can this book be meaningful to us today? How can it fit into our common and contemporary culture? Does Nahum have a message for us? The remarkable thing about the Word of God is that no matter where we turn we find a message for us. Some is specifically directed *to* us, but all of it is *for* us—that is, it has a message for us.

The writer is Nahum, and his name means "comforter," but the message that he gives is one of judgment. How in the world can Nahum live up to his name? How can he be a comforter? Well, it is owing to how you look at the judgment. If it is a judgment upon your enemy, one of whom you are afraid, one who dominates you, then judgment can be a comfort to you.

Nahum is identified in the first verse of the book: "The burden of Nineveh. The book of the vision of Nahum the Elkoshite." Who is an Elkoshite? Well, there are several possible identifications of the city of Elkosh. (1) There was a city of Elkosh in Assyria, a few miles north of the ruins of Nineveh. Nahum could well have lived there and prophesied to Nineveh, as Daniel did to Babylon later on. Very candidly, I do not think that is true; I believe that the content of the book reveals that Nahum did not go to Nineveh. I do not think he was there, nor was he ever called to go there. (2) Another explanation which is offered is that there was a village by the name of Elkosh in Galilee. Jerome recorded that a guide pointed out to him such a village as the birthplace of Nahum. I had that pointed out to me also when I was over there. However, the first time this was ever pointed out was a thousand years after Nahum lived, making such a view largely traditional. Also, Dr. John Davis gives the meaning for Capernaum as "the village of Nahum." If Capernaum is a Hebrew word, then this is the evident origin, and we have no reason to believe otherwise. Nahum was either born there, or he lived there as a boy. (3) Also, down in Judah there was a place called Elkosh. Elkosh seems to have been a common name. We have certain place names in this country of which you will find one in practically every state. You will find a city of the same name in California, in Texas, and then maybe way up in Connecticut. Evidently, Elkosh was a common name like that.

It is the belief of many that what actually happened was that Nahum was born up in the northern kingdom of Israel—which would explain his great attachment to the northern kingdom—but that he later moved down to Elkosh, a place in the south of Judah. He probably went down there as a lad and was raised in the southern kingdom.

The man who wrote this prophecy evidently knew something about Sennacherib's attack upon Jerusalem. It seems to be an eyewitness account that is given in the first chapter. When Sennacherib, king of Assyria, invaded Judah during the reign of Hezekiah, Nahum was probably an eyewitness. This would mean that Nahum was a contemporary of both Isaiah and Micah, and this is the belief of some Bible expositors. I personally have not decided on any definite date at all. There are many dates which have been assigned to this book and this prophet. Dates are suggested anywhere from 720 B.C. to 636 B.C. by conservative scholars. It seems reasonable to locate Nahum about one hundred years after Jonah. He probably lived during the reign of Hezekiah and saw the destruction of the northern kingdom of Israel, and he was greatly moved by that, of course.

Nahum sounds the death knell of Nineveh. He pronounces judgment by the total destruction of Assyria, Nineveh being the capital of that nation. Nahum maintains that God is just in His judgment of this nation.

Actually, I like to study the little Books of Jonah and Nahum together because it was between 100 and 150 years before Nahum appeared on the scene that Jonah went to Nineveh with a message from God. When God told Jonah to go to Nineveh and to bring a message there, a remarkable thing happened—the entire city turned to God—100 percent. Frankly, there has never been anything quite like it in the history of the world. We simply do not seem to have anything else that could compare to an entire city, 100 percent, turning to God. How far-reaching it was in the nation I do not know, but certainly Nineveh, as the capital city, had a tremendous effect upon the nation, and there was a great turning to God in that day.

The question naturally arises: How did it work out? Did it last? Did this nation become a godly nation? And the answer is no—they didn't. In time the revival wore off. In time they went back to their paganism. In time they became as brutal as they had been before. This nation had had a message from God, but now here comes Nahum with another message. I do not think that Nahum actually went to Nineveh. I believe that this man lived in the southern kingdom of Israel, and I don't think he left there. But if God sent Jonah to Nineveh, why did He not send Nahum? Well, God's methods vary. God certainly is immutable—He never changes—but He does change His methods at times. He sent Jonah to Nineveh because Nineveh was a great, wicked city, but they were totally ignorant of God. When the message was brought, the city turned to God, all the way from the king on the throne to the peasant in the hovel. As a result, God spared the city. Now 100 to 150 years have gone by, and the city has relapsed and returned back to its old way. Why doesn't Nahum go? Because they have already had the light, and they've rejected it.

The Lord Jesus spoke about light that is rejected. He said, ". . . If therefore the light that is in thee be darkness, how great is that darkness!" (Matt. 6:23). How can light be darkness in anyone? Light that is darkness is the rejection of the Word of God. There are more Bibles in this country of ours than any other book; it is the best-selling, but least read, book. Assyria was a nation that had had light, but what was the net result? "If therefore the light that is in thee be darkness, how great is that darkness!"

Assyria had had light—God had sent a message to them—and for awhile they turned and served the living and true God. It was a revival in the common sense of the term. It was wonderful, but it didn't last. Isn't that really the history of revivals? At the same time that France had a revolution, England had a revival under the Wesleys and White-field. There was a great turning to God, but how did England make out? Well, look at her today. At that time they were a first-rate nation. They were number one among the great nations of the world, but they are not number one today. They aren't number two; they aren't even number three. They are way down on the list today. What happened? They departed from the living and true God.

The first time I visited England, I asked my guide to take me to the cemetery across from Wesley's church where Wesley is buried. The guide had difficulty. He and the driver talked it over, looked at the city map, and finally wound their way through the streets of London until we arrived at the place. The guide said to me, "This is the first time I've ever brought anyone here. I think I will put it on our route and will bring people here when we take tours. I didn't know it was here." England had forgotten John Wesley. They had forgotten the great revival that took place under him. As a result, she has sunk down to a very low level for a nation which has had such a tremendous history. Those of us who had ancestors in the British Isles—whether in England, Wales, Scotland, or Ireland—have to bow our heads today in shame. We feel like weeping when we think of the greatness of that nation and how at one time they listened to the voice of God. How like Nineveh! When Nineveh was no longer listening, Nahum said, "I'm not going over there. I'm not going to waste my time because there is no point in it. They have passed the point of no return."

And has this nation of mine come to that place today? This little book has a message for us, my friend. Quite a few years ago I cut out this little clipping which reads:

> A United States Senator has stated that the average life of the great civilizations of the world has been about 200 years. He goes on to say that these civilizations have progressed (if that's the right word) through the following stages:
>
> from bondage to spiritual faith
> from spiritual faith to courage
> from courage to liberty
> from liberty to abundance
> from abundance to selfishness
> from selfishness to complacency
> from complacency to apathy
> from apathy back to bondage
>
> The Senator points out the interesting fact that the United States of America will be 200 years old in 12 years. Which of the above stages do you think we're in? How much longer is our civilization going to last?

This nation has now passed its two-hundredth anniversary. Think about this for just a moment. Where are we today? Are we a nation of abundance? Yes, but the Lord is beginning to cut us short. "From abundance to selfishness, from selfishness to complacency"—is that a picture of us today? "From complacency to apathy"—there is an apathetic condition in our nation today. The next step, according to the senator, is "from apathy back to bondage."

This is the picture that is given of Nineveh, and this is the message of Nahum. A great world power, Assyria, with Nineveh as its capital, had a message from God. They turned to God and served God for a period of time. I do not know how long they served Him, but after 100 to 150 years had gone by, they were right back where they were before. Now God is going to judge them. The question arises: Is He right in doing it? Nahum will say that He is not only *right* in doing it, but that He is also *good* when He does it. Some folk think the Book of Nahum should be called "Ho hum"! However, Nahum is a thrilling book to study because it reveals the other side of the attributes of God. God is love, but God is also holy and righteous and good. And God still moves in the lives of nations; therefore, this book speaks right into where we are today.

OUTLINE

CHAPTER 1

THEME: Justice and goodness of God

The little Book of Nahum is a remarkable prophecy. The prophet has just one theme, the judgment of Nineveh, the capital of the Assyrian Empire, but we will find that he also has a meaningful message for us today.

The burden of Nineveh. The book of the vision of Nahum the Elkoshite [Nah. 1:1].

"The burden of Nineveh"—*burden* means "judgment," as it is also used in the prophecy of Isaiah. Earlier, Jonah had brought a message to Nineveh which revealed the *love* of God, and now the message of the Book of Nahum reveals the *justice* of God—the two go together. Although God will judge a nation, He is still love, and He still loves—you cannot escape that. The thing which makes the judgment of God so frightful is the fact that God does not do it as a petulant person. He doesn't do it in a vindictive manner whatsoever. He does not do it in a spirit of revenge or of trying to get even. He does not judge because He has become angry for a moment in a sudden emotional outburst. God judges because He is just. He still loves, but He is just. Since He is just in His dealings, He must deal with sin even in the lives of those whom He loves.

Nineveh was a city that God loved—He told Jonah that. Jonah wanted the city destroyed, but God said, "And should not I spare Nineveh, that great city, wherein are more than sixscore thousand persons that cannot discern between their right hand and their left hand; and also much cattle?" (Jonah 4:11). God wanted to spare the city and the people who were in it, many of whom were little children. And God *had* spared Nineveh, but now judgment is going to fall upon this great city—this is Nahum's message. Jonah, almost a century and a half before, had brought a message from God, and Nineveh had repented. However, the repentance was transitory. God has patiently given this new generation opportunity to repent (see v. 3), but the day of grace now ends and the moment of doom comes. In Nahum 3:19 we read, "There is no healing of thy bruise; thy wound is grievous: all that hear the bruit [news] of thee shall clap the hands over thee: for upon whom hath not thy wickedness passed continually?" In other words, Nineveh has come to a place where there is no healing for her people.

I believe that for a nation and for an individual it is possible to continue in sin until you cross over a mark. I do not know where that mark is—I don't pretend to be able to say when this takes place—but there is such a place. When you pass over that mark, it is not that the grace of God cannot reach you but that you cannot reach God for the simple reason that you have come to the place where you are hardened and in a state of unbelief which cannot be changed. This can be true of a nation, and it can be true of an individual.

As you consider the things which are happening today, you are apt to be discouraged. I am sure that many of God's people are disturbed today. I believe that this is the reason we have had such an interest in prophecy. The wilder the prophetic teachers are, the more popular they seem to be. They are coming up with all kinds of interpretations. The explanation is that God's people, ignorant of the Word of God, are desperately reaching out because of the things which are happening today. The Lord Himself said, "Men's hearts [will be] failing them for fear, and for looking after those things which are coming on the earth: for the powers of heaven shall be shaken" (Luke 21:26). We are at that state for sure; we've come into that particular orbit today. These things are disturbing to us, but, my friend, let us understand that God is still running the affairs of this world. He is still in charge. It hasn't slipped out from His hands. God is not sitting on the edge of His throne, biting His fingernails. He is not nervous today about what is happening. God is carrying out His plan and purpose, and He is overruling the sin of man. This should be very comforting to the child of God in this day.

Assyria had served God's purpose and is now to be destroyed. The destruction of Nineveh, according to the details given in this written prophecy, is almost breathtaking. This is a message, therefore, of comfort to a people who live in fear of a powerful and godless nation: God will destroy any godless nation. All you need do is to pick up your history book and start reading at the beginning of written history. You will find that every great world power went down, and they went down at a time when they were given over to wine, women, and song. When a nation reaches that place, you can be sure that it is on the skids and will soon pass out into the limbo of the lost. That is where all the former great nations of the world are today.

Where is the United States today? We are on the way down, my friend. It is a nice ride while we are having it. Dr. J. Gresham Machen said years ago, "America today is going downhill with a godly ancestry." America, which has had a godly ancestry, is going downhill on a toboggan. And Dr. Machen added, "God pity America when we reach the bottom of the hill." How close are we to the bottom of the hill? I'm no prophet nor the son of a prophet. I'm just a poor preacher, and all I can say is that it seems to me like we're getting very close to the bottom of the hill. The reason that the Book of Nahum is such a remarkable prophecy is that it speaks right into our own situation today.

"The book of the vision of Nahum the Elkoshite." This is all that is known of the writer of this book, and I have discussed this at some length in the Introduction. Nahum was apparently born in the northern kingdom of Israel, and that was his native country; but he moved to the southern part of Judah sometime when he was very young. He had a great concern for the northern kingdom, and he apparently was alive when it was carried away into captivity by Assyria. His message is of the judgment that is coming upon Nineveh.

God is jealous, and the Lord revengeth; the Lord revengeth, and is furious; the Lord will take vengeance on his adversaries, and he reserveth wrath for his enemies [Nah. 1:2].

Jealous, according to Webster's dictionary, means "exacting exclusive devotion." God is a jealous God, and He demands that His people worship Him alone. When any people, no matter who they are, turn to idolatry or turn to sin (all that which is contrary to God), and when they give themselves to it, God is jealous. I hear folk say, "Well, there is just a little bit of difference between the jealousy of God and the jealousy of man." There is not as much difference as you think there is, my friend. In Exodus 20:3–6 we read: "Thou shalt have no other gods before me. Thou shalt not make unto thee any graven image, or any likeness of any thing that is in heaven above, or that is in the earth beneath, or that is in the water under the earth: thou shalt not bow down thyself to them, nor serve them: for I the LORD thy God am a jealous God, visiting the iniquity of the fathers upon the children unto the third and fourth generation of them that hate me; and shewing mercy unto thousands of them that love me, and keep my commandments."

God loves you. It does not make any difference who you are, you cannot keep Him from loving you. You can, however, get into a place where you will not experience the love of God. When you put up an umbrella of sin, the sunshine of God's love will not fall on you, but it is still there for you. You can put up the umbrella of indifference. You can put up the umbrella by turning your back on Him and not doing His will. There are several different umbrellas you can put up that will keep the love of God from shining upon you, but you cannot keep Him from loving you.

Since God loves you, He is actually jealous of you. That means that He wants you. Actually, God doesn't want what you possess. We preachers are always asking you for what you have. I wish that I didn't ever have to mention giving—frankly, I don't like to. If God's people would just give enough to cover our radio broadcasting expenses, you would never hear me mention it. But God doesn't want what you've got—He wants you. And He's jealous when you give yourself, your time, and your substance to other things. When you give yourself to sin, God is jealous.

I once heard a woman say, "I have a very wonderful husband. He's not jealous of me." Well, I don't think that what she said was a compliment at all. We're living in a day when people are supposed to be broad-minded, especially about this matter of sex. They argue that it's all right for a woman to give herself to the first man who comes along.

May I say to you, my friend, if you are that type of woman, you will never get a good husband because the good husband is one who is going to love you and want you above everything else. And he won't want to share you with anybody. If you say that you don't have a jealous husband, I feel sorry for you, because you do not have a good relationship.

God very frankly says, "I'm a jealous God. I want you. I don't want to share you with the sin of the world and with the Devil's crowd and with idolatry. I don't want to share you—I want you to belong to Me." There is nothing wrong with God's saying that He is jealous, and Nahum says, "God is jealous." I'm glad that He is.

Any good wife will say, "I don't want to share my husband with anybody else. He is mine. He belongs to me." This is something which is pretty important today but which the world has forgotten. It is no wonder that in Southern California we have more divorces than marriages. Of course that is what has happened, because people are playing a little game. You used to find the harlots in the brothels; but today it is called "consecutive harlotry," which means that you take one partner at a time, live with him for a little while, and then move on to another. It adds up to the same thing, however. My friend, if you are going to be loved, and if you love, there will be a measure of jealousy in the relationship—there has to be if it is a real love.

"The LORD revengeth; the LORD revengeth, and is furious." The correct translation is not "revengeth," as it is in our Authorized Version—rather, it should be "avengeth." There is a great difference between the two words. ". . . Vengeance is mine; I will repay, saith the LORD" (Rom. 12:19). God says to you and me, "Don't you indulge in vengeance because, to begin with, you will never exercise it in the right way. Turn it over to Me. I handle it without any heat of anger. I handle it in justice. I will do the right thing. And I know all the issues—I know everything about it."

The Lord avengeth; and, whether we like it or not, anything God does is right. We need to get that fixed in our minds and, on the other end of the stick, we need to recognize that you and I are just little creatures who really don't know very much—even the smartest ones don't. Frankly, I hate to say this, but I have quit listening to newscasts and talk programs on which they interview some egghead who is supposed to know something. I've discovered that most of these folk, as far as knowing what really is going on in this world, are ignoramuses who are just talking. We ought to recognize that we don't know much and that whatever God does is *right*. If you don't think so, you are wrong. God is not wrong—you are wrong. I wonder if you are willing to take that position. If you're not, my friend, you're in trouble as far as God is concerned because there are many things He is not going to tell you or me about. He is simply going to go ahead and do them. He is running this universe His way. Oh, I know that we get a few power-hungry human beings, but they don't hang around long. Hitler didn't last long and neither did Mussolini nor Stalin. The others who are on the front page of our newspapers today will be in obituary notices in a few days—it won't be long. May I say to you, God is still on the throne, and He is still running things.

God is "furious." God does not take any delight in the sin of man. God hates sin, and He is furious at it. "The LORD will take vengeance on his adversaries, and he reserveth wrath for his enemies." God is glorified when He judges a nation, as we see especially in Ezekiel 38—39. When Assyria went down, God was glorified in that. They were a brutal, hated, sinful nation, and God brought them down to wrack and ruin and into the debris and dust of the earth. He is glorified when He does things like that. Maybe you don't like it, but the Word of God says that that is the way He moves. I would suggest that you get yourself reconciled to the way God does things, because that is the way they are going to be done.

In verse 3 Nahum puts down a great principle by which God not only judged Assyria (and Nineveh, the capital, in particular), but also the way that God judges the world and will judge the world in the future.

The LORD is slow to anger, and great in power, and will not at all acquit the wicked: the LORD hath his way in the whirlwind and in the storm, and the clouds are the dust of his feet [Nah. 1:3].

"The LORD is slow to anger." Nahum makes this very clear. You see, God had sent Jonah to Nineveh to tell them that they were to be destroyed because of their awful sin. They were known as probably the most brutal people in the ancient world, and God said that judgment would come to them. But the entire city of Nineveh repented and turned to God at that time. Obviously, the message of Jonah penetrated the entire empire, and there was a great change. We would say that a great revival rose up. However, it didn't last very long. It has been characteristic of the great waves of revival which have come that they have never lasted permanently. The Wesleyan revival had tremendous impact upon England and this country, as well as side effects upon other nations, but it was of brief duration. There has been some carry-over from it, of course, even down to the present hour. This is true also of the great revivals under Moody in this country, when entire cities moved toward God. Nahum says that God is slow to anger, but this great city of Nineveh has now turned back to its old ways. One hundred years after Jonah, Nahum comes to say, "The clock has struck twelve, and time has run out. There is no longer any delay. Judgment is coming."

"The LORD . . . will not at all acquit the wicked." The justice of God is seen in His judgment because He is slow to anger. It took Him one hundred years to get around to executing judgment against this city, and He is just and righteous in doing it. He is not going to let the wicked off. Never will He let the wicked off unless they turn to Him. Unless they accept Christ as their Savior because He paid the penalty for their sins, they will have to be judged for their sins. God is not going to let them off—He is just and righteous,

You see, the forgiveness of God is different from our forgiveness. When somebody does us wrong, we say, "I forgive you"—and that's it. A penalty has not been paid. Our forgiveness is generally for something that is just a trifle, although it could be a matter of some importance. But when God forgives, the penalty has already been paid. God is the Judge of this earth. He is not only its Creator, He is not only running it, but He is also the *moral* ruler of this universe. And God is not a crooked judge. You cannot slip something under the table to get Him to let you off easy. You cannot tell Him that you belong to a cer-

tain family, that your father is very influential and will be able to get
you off. Nor can you say you are wealthy and will see that the Judge
loses His job, nor that you will pay Him just a little extra to be lenient
with you. You cannot deal with God like that.

God must judge the wicked, and we are all told that the heart of
man is desperately wicked—not just a little wicked, but desperately
wicked (see Jer. 17:9). You and I do not really know the depths of the
iniquity that is in our hearts; we do not know what we are capable of.
Now God cannot acquit the wicked; therefore, if we are going to be
acquitted, someone must pay the penalty. That is the reason He has
provided a Redeemer for us. When an individual or a nation turns its
back on God's redemption provided now in Christ, then judgment
must follow—there is no other alternative.

"The LORD hath his way in the whirlwind and in the storm, and the
clouds are the dust of his feet." God today moves even in nature. The
storms which come are under His control, and they serve His purpose. So-called Mother Nature doesn't really have anything to do with
it. Mother Nature does what *He* tells Mother Nature to do. Our God is
the Creator, and He is the Redeemer, and He is also the Judge. He's
running things, friend. Just leave it in His hands, and rest in Him
today because He is good, He is gracious, and He is the Savior.

**He rebuketh the sea, and maketh it dry, and drieth up
all the rivers: Bashan languisheth, and Carmel, and the
flower of Lebanon languisheth [Nah. 1:4].**

"He rebuketh the sea, and maketh it dry, and drieth up all the rivers."
God had already shown His power to do this—He dried up the Red
Sea and the Jordan River.

Bashan, Carmel, and Lebanon are the three fertile areas in that
land. Carmel is actually the Valley of Esdraelon, and Megiddo was the
main city there. This is one of the most fertile spots on the topside of
the earth. When you go farther north, along the cost of Lebanon all the
way from Beirut down to the ruins of old Tyre, you see beautiful country. In the spring of the year, you can see the fruit trees blooming and

in the distance the Anti-Lebanons covered with snow. The fruit trees—apricots, peaches, cherries, bananas, and citrus fruit—everything is grown there, and the land is very fertile.

Nahum says that a drought is to come. I am sure there are many of you who remember the dust storms in this country in the 1930s. I have always felt that those storms were a judgment from God. If there had been any kind of a revival at that time, I am confident we would never have had to fight World War II or to have been involved in all that we have since then. But unfortunately, that judgment from God carried no message for this country at that time.

The mountains quake at him, and the hills melt, and the earth is burned at his presence, yea, the world, and all that dwell therein [Nah. 1:5].

He is the Creator, and He's also the Preserver of this universe—He's the One who holds it together.

"The mountains quake at him, and the hills melt" refers, of course, to earthquakes and volcanic eruptions. You can hold Him responsible for anything that takes place, for the floods and the earthquakes that come. But don't hold Him responsible for the people who are killed at that time, because man has been given an intelligence which tells him that he ought not to build too close to a river due to the danger of a flood. Maybe those of us who live here in Southern California ought to listen to Him. We are told that an earthquake is coming, and that is probably true. The San Andreas fault runs very close to where I live, but if an earthquake comes and a loved one of mine is slain by it, I am not going to cry out to God that He is the one who killed him. No—God is not responsible. We would be responsible. We know better. We probably ought to move to another location; but very frankly, my entire family likes Southern California, so we're going to stay right here and take the chance. God does control nature, but you cannot say that He is to blame when these great tragedies take place. Man is responsible for them. He ought not to get too close to a river, and he ought to stay away from where he knows there are going to be earthquakes.

Who can stand before his indignation? and who can abide in the fierceness of his anger? his fury is poured out like fire, and the rocks are thrown down by him [Nah. 1:6].

Man has learned that you cannot stand up against nature. Victor Hugo wrote three great novels. He wrote *Les Misérables* to show that society is the enemy of man; he wrote *The Hunchback of Notre Dame* to show that religion is the enemy of man; and he wrote *The Toilers of the Sea* to show that nature is the enemy of man. Well, it is owing to how man approaches each of these. Religion has been an enemy of man. Society is the enemy of man—this civilization today is no friend of grace, I can assure you of that. It is true that nature can be an enemy of man, but it can also be his friend. The issue is that if you are going to try to fight against nature, you're fighting a losing battle. This is what Victor Hugo tried to show in his novel.

"Who can stand before his indignation? and who can abide in the fierceness of his anger?" This question was directed to the people of Nineveh who had rejected the mercy of this all-powerful God. Do *you* have the answer to that question? I'd like to ask that of you if you are unsaved. Maybe you are depending upon your own righteousness and goodness. Do you really believe that you can stand in the presence of a holy God who absolutely hates sin and intends to judge it? Are you able to stand in His holy presence?

The very brilliant Oxford don, C. S. Lewis, wrote a story in which he tells about a bus trip that was run from hell to heaven. It was the sort of tour in which those who were in hell could take a bus trip to heaven. The bus was filled and, when it arrived in heaven, the driver parked the bus in a parking lot (I'm sure there is plenty of parking space up there). The driver told everyone on the bus, "At four o'clock this afternoon, the bus is going to leave and head for home." Home just happened to be hell. And at four o'clock that afternoon, the bus was filled—everyone was back. The bus driver told them, "If you want to stay, you can stay." Why didn't they stay? It was because they had found out they had no place in heaven. One of the great saints of the past put it this way: "I would rather go to hell without sin than go to heaven with sin."

"Who can stand before his indignation?" If you don't have a Savior, how are you going to stand as a sinner in the presence of a holy God? Do you think that you've got a chance? You don't have a ghost of a chance, my friend. You cannot stand there without a Savior. To be able to stand in His presence is what it means to be accepted into the beloved and to be in Christ. This is a tremendous principle that Nahum is putting down here. God must judge sin. There is something radically wrong with God if He doesn't judge sin.

Nahum's description of the power and the anger of God was to reassure the people of Judah of the protection of their all-powerful God when Assyria would invade their land.

> **The LORD is good, a strong hold in the day of trouble;**
> **and he knoweth them that trust in him [Nah. 1:7].**

"The LORD is good." Let's keep that in mind. Remember that the psalmist said, "O give thanks unto the LORD, for he is good: for his mercy endureth for ever. Let the redeemed of the LORD say so . . ." (Ps. 107:1–2). If the redeemed don't say so, nobody's going to say so. So I am going to say so: God is good. God is good, friend—that's wonderful to know. I do not know who you are, where you are, or how you are, but I do know that God loves you and He wants to save you. If you are not saved, it is simply because you will not come to Him, for He can save you and He will save you. God is good—that is an axiom of Scripture and an axiom of life. "The LORD is good."

"A strong hold in the day of trouble." Are you having any trouble? Do you want to get to a good shelter? The Lord is that shelter which you need.

"And he knoweth them that trust in him." I'm very happy that I'm not going to get lost in the shuffle, that I won't get lost in the multitudes. As I travel from city to city, I sometimes think that everyone has moved to the West Coast. I get on one of our freeways here, and I think, *My, how many people there are!* But then I go back to Dallas,

Texas, and I think that everyone has followed me from California to
Texas! The crowds are everywhere. I go to Florida or to New York City,
and it seems the people have followed me there. I have never seen
such crowds in my life! I went to Europe several years ago and found
that the people were there also! The multitudes which are in the Ori-
ent almost shock us. And in Egypt, in the Arab countries, and in Tur-
key there are multitudes of people. It causes me to think, *My, I hope
the Lord remembers that my name is Vernon McGee and that I have
trusted Him.* I am very happy that the Scripture says, "He knoweth
them that trust in him." My friend, He doesn't need a computer to
record your name. Actually, He has you written on His heart; He's
written your name on the palms of His hands. He knows you—He
knows those who have trusted Him.

> **But with an overrunning flood he will make an utter
> end of the place thereof, and darkness shall pursue his
> enemies [Nah. 1:8].**

The Lord will overwhelm and destroy the Assyrians. "An overrun-
ning flood" pictures a river that is overflowing its banks and causing
devastation as it moves. It is believed that this refers to the invading
army of the Babylonians which overcame Nineveh. The Greek historian Ctesias of the fifth century B.C. records that the Babylonian army
was able to invade Nineveh when the Tigris River suddenly over-
flowed and washed away the floodgates of the city and the foundations of the palace.

"Darkness shall pursue his enemies" raises a question in my mind
regarding the place of permanent punishment. There is more said in
Scripture about darkness being the lot of the lost than there is about
fire. Darkness is mentioned here—"and darkness shall pursue his enemies." Even the Lord Jesus used the term: "But the children of the
kingdom shall be cast out into outer darkness: there shall be weeping
and gnashing of teeth" (Matt. 8:12; see also Matt. 22:13). Literal fire
could only affect the physical, never the spiritual. But, oh, the fires of
a conscience that has been suddenly alerted to the awful thing one did
in rejecting Christ and in not doing the things he should have done.

Think of the darkness of a lost eternity! Think of not being able to see where you are going at all. Darkness, to me, is a better and more fearful description of hell than fire is. That may be a new thought for you, and I would urge you to pursue it in the Word of God.

GOD'S DECISION TO DESTROY NINEVEH AND TO GIVE THE GOSPEL

What do ye imagine against the LORD? he will make an utter end: affliction shall not rise up the second time [Nah. 1:9].

"What do ye imagine against the LORD?" Nahum puts this question directly to the Assyrian invaders. In effect he is asking, as Dr. Charles Feinberg has stated it, "Can you cope with such a God as Israel has?"

"He will make an utter end"—that is, the Assyrian power will be completely destroyed. It will give you a better understanding of this to read the fulfillment in the historical account in Isaiah 37.

"Affliction shall not rise up the second time." In other words, Nineveh will not be given a second chance. They have had their last chance. They've crossed over that invisible line—I do not know where it is, but it is there somewhere, and you can step over it in your rejection of God. This does not mean that the grace of God could not reach you but that you can no longer reach it after you have come to that particular point.

For while they be folden together as thorns, and while they are drunken as drunkards, they shall be devoured as stubble fully dry [Nah. 1:10].

"For while they be folden together as thorns" probably describes the Assyrian army, which presented such a united front that they seemed like entangled thorns—impossible to break through.

"While they are drunken as drunkards, they shall be devoured as stubble fully dry." God would completely destroy them. The fulfillment of this is recorded in Isaiah 37:36–37.

I would say this especially to young people today: Make your decision for Christ while you are young and have a sharp mind. You can keep playing around with intellectualism (which I tried in college and almost got detoured), or you can play around as many are doing with drugs and alcohol, but Nahum says that the day will come when you will stumble around like a drunkard. If you stumble around like a drunkard, you cannot make a decision. A man who had been drinking called me the other night from back east. I refused to talk with him. I told him, "The liquor is speaking and not you. When you are willing to sober up, call me, and I'll be glad to talk with you, but I will not talk to liquor." May I say to you, Nineveh had reached the place where they could make no decision.

Along with the other minor prophets, Nahum makes a contribution to God's philosophy of government and His manner of dealing with individuals and with nations. The point Nahum is going to make is that whether you believe it or not, whether you can understand it or not, God is just and God is good when He judges a nation or an individual. God is still the God of love. He loves the lost. He is, as the apostle John tells us, ". . . the propitiation [the mercy seat] for our sins: and not for ours only, but also for the sins of the whole world" (1 John 2:2).

Men are lost because they are sinners, and they are saved because they accept the overture of salvation that God extends to them. God will get that invitation to any individual on the topside of this earth who will accept it. I have come to believe that we may see a turning to God. I do not mean in great numbers, but I believe there will be a turning to God in response to the invitation given to every people on the topside of this earth. It looks to me right now that radio broadcasting will be the means of bringing that invitation to the unreached.

Nahum is going to be very extreme in what he says. God is going to judge Nineveh, and He is just and righteous in doing it. But God is love also. His judgment is actually an act of His love—that is very difficult for us to comprehend, but it is absolutely true.

There is one come out of thee, that imagineth evil against the LORD, a wicked counsellor [Nah. 1:11].

Nahum says now that there had come up against Judah this enemy—the enemy is Assyria with its capital city of Nineveh. I think that there is agreement among all conservative Bible expositors that the invader that is spoken of here as "a wicked counsellor" was Sennacherib, the king of Assyria. This invasion by Sennacherib is recorded three times in Scripture: in 2 Kings 18—19; 2 Chronicles 32; and also in Isaiah 36—37. When God says something three times, we ought to stop, look, and listen. When He says it once, that should be enough. When He says it twice—sometimes He says, "Verily, verily, I say unto you"—it is extra important. But when He repeats something three times, you can just put it down that it is all-important.

Nahum is referring now to this wicked counselor who had come against Jerusalem. We read in the historical accounts that Sennacherib sent Rabshakeh against Jerusalem with the great army of Assyria. Rabshakeh threatened Hezekiah, the king of Judah, and Hezekiah was almost frightened to death by it all. I think that poor man probably couldn't sleep at night during that period of time. However, Hezekiah went into the temple and called upon God, and then the prophet Isaiah brought the message that Rabshakeh would not even shoot an arrow into the city of Jerusalem. Instead, he had to withdraw because of Assyria's campaign against Egypt in which Sennacherib needed his reinforcements. Then God Himself *destroyed* the army of the Assyrians! Assyria was greatly feared in Judah since during that period they had taken the northern kingdom of Israel into captivity and had dealt with them in a very brutal manner.

> **Thus saith the LORD; Though they be quiet, and likewise many, yet thus shall they be cut down, when he shall pass through. Though I have afflicted thee, I will afflict thee no more [Nah. 1:12].**

This is a rather remarkable verse, and we do not want to miss the point that is here. This expression, "Though they be quiet, and likewise many," does not quite make sense to me. What is it that God is saying here?

I know most of the men who worked as editors on *The New Sco-*

field Reference Bible, and all of them are just as human as you and I are. They are subject to mistakes and not one of them, as far as I know, feels that their notes were inspired. However, every now and then, they have really put in a helpful note. Their note on this verse is an example of how archaeology has confirmed many things in Scripture that we would not have known or understood otherwise, thus revealing the accuracy of the Word of God. *The New Scofield Reference Bible* (pp. 950–951) uses the following note on verse 12:

> In the context the expression "quiet, and likewise many," although a literal translation of the Hebrew, does not seem to make much sense. Actually the Hebrew here represents a transliteration of a long-forgotten Assyrian legal formula. Excavation in the ruins of ancient Ninevah, buried since 612 B.C., has brought to light thousands of ancient Assyrian tablets, dozens of which contain this Assyrian legal formula. It proves, on investigation, to indicate joint and several responsibility for carrying out an obligation. Nahum quotes the LORD as using this Assyrian formula in speaking to the Assyrians, saying in effect, "Even though your entire nation joins as one person to resist me, nevertheless I shall overcome you." As the words would have been equally incomprehensible to the later Hebrew copyists, their retention is striking evidence of the care of the scribes in copying exactly what they found in the manuscripts, and testifies to God's providential preservation of the Bible text.

Therefore, you can see that God used an Assyrian legal formula in expressing what He wanted to say. He was talking about Assyria, and He wanted them to understand what He was saying. When we look at this verse in light of what archaeology has discovered today, God was saying something that made sense to the Assyrians although it does not make sense to us today. When the Hebrew scholars came along, they didn't know what this meant either, but they translated it literally into English because they believed in the plenary, verbal inspiration of the Scriptures. Thank God for that!

This leads me to say that this is one of the reasons I cannot approve of a lot of these so-called modern translations. They are not translations at all because many of them were done by men who do not believe that the Bible is the Word of God. Other men, although they believe it is the Word of God, have wanted to put it into a form that modern man could understand. I rather disagree with that method. I am very happy that The Living Bible calls itself "a paraphrased text." I would say concerning The Living Bible that it is a bad translation, but in many places it is a marvelous paraphrased text. If you will treat it as a paraphrase, that's fine, but do not believe that you are getting the literal text of Scripture.

This passage here in Nahum reveals that, although you might not understand something in Scripture, God says, "You take it as I have given it to you, and you will find out someday what it means—that is, if you will work and study hard enough." The trouble is that we are trying to make the Word of God like pabulum, and we are trying to spoon-feed a bunch of babies who are too lazy to really study the Word of God. Although I certainly am one who is accused of making the Word of God simple, I do believe that there ought to be a real reverence for the text of Scripture. I'm no Bible worshiper, I'm no bibliophile, by any means, but I do believe that there should be a reverence for the text of Scripture.

I have spent time on this verse because it contains this expression that I did not understand until this archaeological discovery was made. Archaeology has done a great deal of work yonder at the ancient city of Nineveh. The tell of Nineveh, across the Tigris River from the modern city of Mosul, was first excavated in the last century.

For now will I break his yoke from off thee, and will burst thy bonds in sunder [Nah. 1:13].

This seemed impossible in the day when Nahum wrote it because the nation of Assyria was to continue for a long time yet. But God said at that time, "I am going to break the yoke of this nation."

He also said:

> And the LORD hath given a commandment concerning
> thee, that no more of thy name be sown: out of the house
> of thy gods will I cut off the graven image and the molten
> image: I will make thy grave; for thou art vile [Nah.
> 1:14].

What God says to Nineveh is harsh. He says, "I'm going to bury you."
Nikita Khrushchev wasn't the first one who used that expression; he
said that to the people of the United States, and it seemed very terrifying to us, naturally. Actually, Khrushchev was using a biblical expression, but he didn't know it. God said to Nineveh, "I'm going to bury
you, and when I bury you, you'll go out of business as a nation." When
was the last time you saw an Assyrian running around? There are not
many, and they have no nation today. God said to them, "I'll bury
you," and that is what He did.

He also said, "I'm going to get rid of your gods, that is, your idolatry." It was the Medes and the Babylonians who eventually came and
destroyed the city of Nineveh in 612 B.C. The Assyrian idolatry was
destroyed by the Medes who were a monotheistic people and did not
worship idols. They were really iconoclasts, and they broke up the
idolatry of Assyria.

> Behold upon the mountains the feet of him that bringeth
> good tidings, that publisheth peace! O Judah, keep thy
> solemn feasts, perform thy vows: for the wicked shall no
> more pass through thee; he is utterly cut off [Nah. 1:15].

God is saying through Nahum, "Don't leave Me. Don't withdraw from
the Mosaic system. Don't give it up, because I intend to destroy your
enemy and to send to you the Messiah, who will bring tidings of great
joy."

Nahum says this in reference to Assyria, and you will find that
Isaiah actually uses the same expression in Isaiah 52:7, where it is
amplified: "How beautiful upon the mountains are the feet of him that
bringeth good tidings, that publisheth peace; that bringeth good
tidings of good, that publisheth salvation; that saith unto Zion, Thy

God reigneth!" Isaiah spoke this in reference to the destruction of Babylon as he wrote to the southern kingdom of Judah. Nahum, writing to the northern kingdom, says the same thing but concerning Assyria. Then notice that Paul quotes this in his Epistle to the Romans: "For whosoever shall call upon the name of the Lord shall be saved. How then shall they call on him in whom they have not believed? and how shall they believe in him of whom they have not heard? and how shall they hear without a preacher? And how shall they preach, except they be sent? as it is written, How beautiful are the feet of them that preach the gospel of peace, and bring glad tidings of good things!" (Rom. 10:13–15).

I think Nahum was the first to say this and then Isaiah. Finally, Paul quotes Isaiah and makes a different application of it in the section of his epistle that refers to Israel, that is, in the dispensational section of Romans. Paul is arguing there that God is not through with the nation Israel and that in the future there will again come to them the good tidings of great joy. But it is also a worldwide message that is applicable to today. Paul writes, "For whosoever shall call upon the name of the Lord shall be saved" (Rom. 10:13).

But how will people hear without somebody bringing the message to them? The messengers must be sent, and I believe that God will do the sending. Isaiah wrote, "How beautiful upon the mountains are the feet of him that bringeth good tidings . . ." (Isa. 52:7). That's not because they have beautiful feet, but because they have come to bring the message of the gospel. They may have traveled by boat, or they may have come by plane, or they may have come by radio, but they have come bringing the message. In our radio ministry we believe that the gospel should begin here at our own Jerusalem, and therefore we are attempting to continue to reach this country with the Word of God as well as we can. But we want also to go right to the ends of the earth via radio. Very frankly, I want my feet to be beautiful, and I want my feet to be ". . . shod with the preparation of the gospel of peace" (Eph. 6:15). I want to walk all over this earth by radio, and I want to reach out to folk with the Good News today.

This is a marvelous way in which the Spirit of God uses Scripture. You get a good course in hermeneutics (the methods of interpretation of Scripture) when you read the little Book of Nahum. Nahum tells you how to interpret the Word of God. He has already shown us that we are to take it literally whether we understand it or not. There is an explanation, and the trouble is not with the Word of God; the trouble is with us when we do not understand it. Then we have also seen that God made direct interpretation of this Scripture to one nation at one time, to another nation at another time, and it now has a worldwide application today.

CHAPTER 2

THEME: Execution of God's decision to destroy
Nineveh

In chapters 2—3 we are going to see the justice and goodness of God
exhibited in the execution of His decision to destroy Nineveh. God
didn't just talk about destroying Nineveh—God did it, and He did it
in a very remarkable way.

ANNIHILATION OF ASSYRIA

In chapter 2 Nahum prophesies a frightful judgment upon Assyria,
and history testifies to its literal fulfillment. God has made it very
clear in chapter 1 where He says, "I will make thy grave; for thou art
vile" (Nah. 1:14); in other words, He says to Assyria, "I'm going to
bury you." And, believe me, that is exactly what happened.

> **He that dasheth in pieces is come up before thy face:
> keep the munition, watch the way, make thy loins
> strong, fortify thy power mightily [Nah. 2:1].**

This refers to the Medo-Babylonian forces that came against Assyria
and destroyed it in 612 B.C. under the leadership of Cyaxares and
Nabopolassar. It is very interesting that Nahum, with biting sarcasm,
tells Assyria, "You sure had better fortify yourself." The Assyrians
spared no one, and they thought that their capital was impregnable
and that they could withstand any kind of a judgment. But God is
saying to this nation, "You are going to be destroyed."

> **For the LORD hath turned away the excellency of Jacob,
> as the excellency of Israel: for the emptiers have emptied
> them out, and marred their vine branches [Nah. 2:2].**

Nahum is saying that the time has come for Assyria's judgment because God has completed the judgment of His own people and intends to restore them. The mention of both "Jacob" and "Israel" is a reference to both the southern kingdom of Judah and the northern kingdom of Israel. "The emptiers" are the enemies of God's people, especially the nation of Assyria. The "vine branches" is probably a symbol of the nation of Israel (see Ps. 80:8–16).

This chapter is Nahum's detailed prophecy, which today is an accurate, historical record of what took place about one hundred years after Nahum. It speaks of the finality of the judgment of God upon the nation of Assyria; it speaks of the fact that Assyria would never make a comeback. Assyria never did make a comeback, and she never will. According to the Word of God, Babylon will resurge as well as some other nations. But Assyria, one of the great powers in the ancient world, will not make a comeback—God makes that very, very clear.

The capture of Nineveh is described here in rather lurid terms. This passage reveals just how terrible it was, and you could write over this chapter, ". . . whatsoever a man soweth, that shall he also reap" (Gal. 6:7). Assyria had been a very brutal nation, one of the most brutal nations the world has ever seen. For example, one of the things which the Assyrians did to an enemy was to bury him out in the desert sand right up to his chin. Then they would put a thong through his tongue and leave him out in the hot blazing sun, first to go mad, and then to die. That was one of the "nice little things" the Assyrians came up with. They also had several other little surprises for their enemies. It is said that when the Assyrians were on the march, in many places an entire community which lay in the line of their march would commit suicide rather than fall into the hands of brutal Assyrians. They were dreaded and feared in the ancient world. We find here in the Book of Nahum that Assyria is again beginning to move, but now their movement is in retreat. They are no longer the aggressor, but the Medes and the Babylonians are coming up against them.

The shield of his mighty men is made red, the valiant men are in scarlet: the chariots shall be with flaming

**torches in the day of his preparation, and the fir trees
shall be terribly shaken [Nah. 2:3].**

"The shield of his mighty men is made red." This does not mean that
their shields were made red with blood as some have suggested. The
Assyrians were especially fond of the color of red, or scarlet. In all of
their art, the color red is frequently found, and they evidently were
very much interested in it. They made everything red. Some scholars
believe that they used copper shields and that the reflection of the
sunlight on the copper appeared red. Why did they do this? It is believed that they did this to frighten their enemies. As you well know,
in warfare you intend to do as much bluffing as you do fighting. You
want to frighten your enemies as much as you possibly can.

In World War II, when the United States issued a warning before
the atom bomb was dropped, the Japanese thought that America was
bluffing. That was one time when we were not bluffing, but they did
not pay any attention to our warning at all. Today there are many who
are using the crying towel, who flagellate this nation, declaring that
we are guilty of this awful thing. I personally do not feel that our
nation should go into sackcloth and ashes because of what we did at
that time. It was an awful, horrible thing, but after all, war is a very
awful, horrible thing. Our boys were being slain, and we were not
winning the war by any means. The dropping of the bomb was what
brought the war to an end, and my feeling is that we were justified in
it. But I am also very frank to say that we see God's principle working
out here in the Book of Nahum, that this enemy who was so brutal
reaped exactly what they sowed. I do not think it will be any different
with the United States. We happened to be the first ones to drop an
atom bomb, and I am not sure that God is going to forget that.

The whole point is that in warfare you do attempt to bluff your
enemy, and that is probably the reason the Assyrians used the color
red. "The valiant men are in scarlet"—again we have the color red,
you see. The Assyrians had uniforms which were red.

"The chariots shall be with flaming torches in the day of his preparation, and the fir trees shall be terribly shaken." This refers to the

armor that was on the chariots and the way in which they were built. The Assyrian chariots were not built of wood like the chariots you see in the museum in Cairo, Egypt. The Egyptians used a great deal of wood in building their chariots, but apparently the Assyrians were the ones who got the latest model in chariots. They were sort of the General Motors of chariot building.

> **The chariots shall rage in the streets, they shall justle one against another in the broad ways: they shall seem like torches, they shall run like the lightnings [Nah. 2:4].**

Verse 4 will illustrate to us a method of interpretation of Scripture which is entirely wrong. Let me just say that Nahum is talking here about the battle between the chariots of the Assyrians and the chariots of the enemy. What happened was that when the enemy came against Assyria, they faced the well-defended city of Nineveh. Diodorus Siculus, a Greek historian, tells us that Nineveh had fifteen hundred towers, each of which was two hundred feet high. But at the time of the siege, the Tigris River rose up and flooded, and it took out an entire section of the wall of the city. The river did what the enemy could not do—it breached the walls of Nineveh. Then the enemy was able to come in and penetrate the city itself. They opened the canals used for irrigation and thus flooded the palace. This is the way in which the enemy was able to take the city. The breach in the wall was so great that the chariots of the enemy could get in, and what is described in verse 4 is nothing in the world but the chariot battle which took place at that time.

There is a type of interpretation of prophecy which I deplore, and I regret that at the present hour we see so much of it. For example, there are those who say that this verse is a prophecy of the automobile! That is what Sir Robert Anderson calls "the wild utterances of prophecy mongers." There is a great interest in prophecy today because great world events and world crises are taking place. But we need to recognize that we can become fanatical and go overboard concerning prophecy. I believe it was Winston Churchill who said, "A fanatic is one who cannot change his mind, and he won't change the subject." Some folk today are just dwelling on prophecy (after all, it is a limited subject), and they become fanatical in their interpretations.

My friend, I do not think you could even make that kind of application of it for the very simple reason that automobiles don't rage in the streets. To tell the truth, sometimes the drivers rage when they get tied up in traffic, but the automobiles don't rage. Sometimes an automobile manages to stay right where it is and not move at all when it gets a vapor lock! And automobiles do not "justle one against another in the broad ways." Actually, when one jostles against another, it means you have a wreck. One New Year's Eve, as I was out on the freeways of Southern California with a friend, we saw one wreck after another. The apparently there were quite a few drunk drivers out that evening. The point is that automobiles don't jostle one against another.

What is Nahum talking about when he says, "The chariots shall rage in the streets, they shall justle one against another in the broad ways"? Well, if you have ever been in a museum which had some of the Assyrian relics, you have perhaps seen that on the chariot wheels, that is, on the hub of the wheels, there was a sharp blade. It was like a sword or a sickle, a very dangerous instrument which extended out from the wheel. The one driving the chariot would go up as close as he could get to the enemy, and this very sharp instrument would cut off the wooden wheel of the enemy's chariot. It would put a chariot out of business right away if you could cut off the wheel on one side. That is the jostling together that Nahum mentions here, and it hasn't anything to do with the automobile!

"They shall seem like torches, they shall run like the lightnings." The chariots moved very fast in that day, although in our day it would seem very slow. The Assyrians had developed the art of fighting by chariot to a very fine degree, and the enemy had picked that up so that when they clashed in the broad ways of the city and outside the city, the battle was a frightful, horrible thing. That, my friend, is all that Nahum is talking about here.

I believe that you can make moral and spiritual applications from the Word of God, but I don't think that you can take this prophecy and

The gates of the rivers shall be opened, and the palace shall be dissolved [Nah. 2:6].

Nahum prophesies here that the Tigris River will be turned into the city. At the time this campaign was carried on, the heavy rains in that area caused the Tigris River to reach flood stage. The floodwaters took out a section of the wall, and the city became like a pool of water. "The gates of the rivers shall be opened, and the palace shall be dissolved." I think that the foundations of the palace were swept out and that the water absolutely brought the palace down. Secular history tells us that part of the city wall was taken out. About 2½ miles of the wall of Nineveh was right along by the side of the Tigris River. The city was situated well above the normal flow of the river, but with the river at flood stage, it took out a whole section of the wall, and the enemy was able to enter the city. In other words, the overflowing river ma[de] breach that the enemy was attempting to make them[selves] seem as though the Lord cooperated in the de[struction] floodgates were opened, and even the pa[lace] flooding. We are told that the enemy open[ed] the palace was completely inundated wit[h]

And Huzzab shall be led away ca[ptive] brought up, and her maids shall le[ad her as with the] voice of doves, tabering upon their b[reasts]

Huzzab literally means "it is decreed." This v[erse] it is decreed, she shall be led away captive, sh[e] and her maids shall lead her as with the voice [of doves] beating] upon their breasts." I used to hunt dove[s] fellow. Late in the afternoon, we would hunt dov[es] been put up and there was a body of water used cattle—we called it a tank in those days. The birds late in the afternoon, and as we would come up over we'd be able to get a good shot at the doves. They wo[uld] and the flapping of their wings would be like the s upon your chest. This is the picture that is given to us interpret it in a literal way for our day. Do you see what a remarkable book Nahum is? We have here another great principle for interpreting the Word of God. For example, when you read in Isaiah, ". . . therefore shalt thou plant pleasant plants, and shalt set it with strange slips" (Isa. 17:10), you cannot interpret that to mean the orange trees which today abound in that land. The natural habitat of the orange tree is the land of Israel. In fact, that whole area grew oranges way back even in the days of Solomon. When Solomon speaks in the Song of Solomon of dwelling under the apple tree, the "apple" referred to is actually a citron fruit, probably an orange tree (see Song 2:3). My point is that we cannot take Scriptures that have an interpretation for a different people at a different time and try to bring them up-to-date and interpret them for our own day.

I want to mention again that the little Books of Jonah and Nahum go together. What you have in the Book of Jonah is actually not a prophecy but rather an account of Jonah's missionary activity in the city of Nineveh when the total population turned to God and God spared them from judgment. But time went by, and they departed from the Lord again. One hundred years after Jonah, God raised up Nahum, and his entire message is directed against Nineveh. What we have, therefore, in the Book of Nahum is a very vivid prophecy of the total annihilation of this city. The city was so completely destroyed that it was not until 1850 that the site of Nineveh was located and excavated. A great deal has been learned about the city of Nineveh and the Assyrian civilization through that excavation.

He shall recount his worthies: they shall stumble in their walk; they shall make haste to the wall th[ere]of, and the defence shall be prepared [Nah.

The destruction of Nineveh [...]
the city under Cya[xares ...]
kingdom b[...]

The beating upon their breast was just like the noise made by doves taking flight. The dove's call, by the way, is a mourning noise, and that is the reason it is called the mourning dove. I have been told that that mourning noise is actually the love call of the dove.

But Nineveh is of old like a pool of water; yet they shall flee away. Stand, stand, shall they cry; but none shall look back [Nah. 2:8].

"But Nineveh is of old like a pool of water." The flood had entered, and the city became like a lake.

"Stand, stand, shall they cry; but none shall look back." The command was given to them to hold their ground, but when they saw the flood coming in along with the enemy, they decided it was time not to listen to their commanders but to turn and run away as fast as possible.

Take ye the spoil of silver, take the spoil of gold: for there is none end of the store and glory out of all the pleasant furniture [Nah. 2:9].

"Take ye the spoil of silver, take the spoil of gold." The enemy is invited to take the spoil of silver and to take the spoil of gold. "For there is none end of the store and glory out of all the pleasant furniture." The city of Nineveh was very wealthy and highly ornate. The palaces were beautiful, and the people lived in luxury because of the success they had had in warfare. You see, the Assyrians had brought in booty from all of the great nations of that day—even the southern kingdom of Judah was paying tribute to them at that time—so that the city had become very wealthy.

She is empty, and void, and waste: and the heart melteth, and the knees smite together, and much pain is in all loins, and the faces of them all gather blackness [Nah. 2:10].

one who cannot change his mind, and he won't change the subject."
Some folk today are just dwelling on prophecy (after all, it is a limited
subject), and they become fanatical in their interpretations.

My friend, this prophecy has nothing in the world to do with the
automobile. I do not think you could even make that kind of application of it for the very simple reason that automobiles don't rage in the
streets. To tell the truth, sometimes the drivers rage when they get tied
up in traffic, but the automobiles don't rage. Sometimes an automobile manages to stay right where it is and not move at all when it gets a
vapor lock! And automobiles do not "justle one against another in the
broad ways." Actually, when one jostles against another, it means you
have a wreck. One New Year's Eve, as I was out on the freeways of
Southern California with a friend, we saw one wreck after another—
apparently there were quite a few drunk drivers out that evening. The
point is that automobiles don't jostle one against another.

What *is* Nahum talking about when he says, "The chariots shall
rage in the streets, they shall justle one against another in the broad
ways"? Well, if you have ever been in a museum which had some of
the Assyrian relics, you have perhaps seen that on the chariot wheels,
that is, on the hub of the wheels, there was a sharp blade. It was like a
sword or a sickle, a very dangerous instrument which extended out
from the wheel. The one driving the chariot would go up as close as
he could get to the enemy, and this very sharp instrument would cut
off the wooden wheel of the enemy's chariot. It would put a chariot
out of business right away if you could cut off the wheel on one side.
That is the jostling together that Nahum mentions here, and it hasn't
anything to do with the automobile!

"They shall seem like torches, they shall run like the lightnings."
The chariots moved very fast in that day, although in our day it would
seem very slow. The Assyrians had developed the art of fighting by
chariot to a very fine degree, and the enemy had picked that up so that
when they clashed in the broad ways of the city and outside the city,
the battle was a frightful, horrible thing. That, my friend, is all that
Nahum is talking about here.

I believe that you can make moral and spiritual applications from
the Word of God, but I don't think that you can take this prophecy and

interpret it in a literal way for our day. Do you see what a remarkable book Nahum is? We have here another great principle for interpreting the Word of God. For example, when you read in Isaiah, ". . . therefore shalt thou plant pleasant plants, and shalt set it with strange slips" (Isa. 17:10), you cannot interpret that to mean the orange trees which today abound in that land. The natural habitat of the orange tree is the land of Israel. In fact, that whole area grew oranges way back even in the days of Solomon. When Solomon speaks in the Song of Solomon of dwelling under the apple tree, the "apple" referred to is actually a *citron* fruit, probably an orange tree (see Song 2:3). My point is that we cannot take Scriptures that have an interpretation for a different people at a different time and try to bring them up-to-date and interpret them for our own day.

I want to mention again that the little Books of Jonah and Nahum go together. What you have in the Book of Jonah is actually not a prophecy but rather an account of Jonah's missionary activity in the city of Nineveh when the total population turned to God and God spared them from judgment. But time went by, and they departed from the Lord again. One hundred years after Jonah, God raised up Nahum, and his entire message is directed against Nineveh. What we have, therefore, in the Book of Nahum is a very vivid prophecy of the total annihilation of this city. The city was so completely destroyed that it was not until 1850 that the site of Nineveh was located and excavated. A great deal has been learned about the city of Nineveh and the Assyrian civilization through that excavation.

He shall recount his worthies: they shall stumble in their walk; they shall make haste to the wall thereof, and the defence shall be prepared [Nah. 2:5].

The destruction of Nineveh came about when the Medes came against the city under Cyaxares. Babylon at that time was not the greatest kingdom, but they did join with the Medes in this battle.

The king of Assyria depended upon his military leaders, but because of their fear, they stumbled and fell in their march. Of course, the defense of the city's wall was of primary importance in the battle.

The gates of the rivers shall be opened, and the palace shall be dissolved [Nah. 2:6].

Nahum prophesies here that the Tigris River will be turned into the city. At the time this campaign was carried on, the heavy rains in that area caused the Tigris River to reach flood stage. The floodwaters took out a section of the wall, and the city became like a pool of water. "The gates of the rivers shall be opened, and the palace shall be dissolved." I think that the foundations of the palace were swept out and that the water absolutely brought the palace down. Secular history tells us that part of the city wall was taken out. About 2½ miles of the wall of Nineveh was right along by the side of the Tigris River. The city was situated well above the normal flow of the river, but with the river at flood stage, it took out a whole section of the wall, and the enemy was able to enter the city. In other words, the overflowing river made the breach that the enemy was attempting to make themselves. It would seem as though the Lord cooperated in the destruction of the city. The floodgates were opened, and even the palace was brought down by the flooding. We are told that the enemy opened the irrigation ditches and the palace was completely inundated with water.

And Huzzab shall be led away captive, she shall be brought up, and her maids shall lead her as with the voice of doves, tabering upon their breasts [Nah. 2:7].

Huzzab literally means "it is decreed." This verse should read, "And it is decreed, she shall be led away captive, she shall be brought up, and her maids shall lead her as with the voice of doves, tabering [or, *beating*] upon their breasts." I used to hunt doves in Texas as a young fellow. Late in the afternoon, we would hunt down where a dam had been put up and there was a body of water used for the watering of cattle—we called it a tank in those days. The birds would come there late in the afternoon, and as we would come up over the embankment, we'd be able to get a good shot at the doves. They would all take flight, and the flapping of their wings would be like the sound of beating upon your chest. This is the picture that is given to us here by Nahum.

The beating upon their breast was just like the noise made by doves taking flight. The dove's call, by the way, is a mourning noise, and that is the reason it is called the mourning dove. I have been told that that mourning noise is actually the love call of the dove.

> **But Nineveh is of old like a pool of water: yet they shall flee away. Stand, stand, shall they cry; but none shall look back [Nah. 2:8].**

"But Nineveh is of old like a pool of water." The flood had entered, and the city became like a lake.

"Stand, stand, shall they cry; but none shall look back." The command was given to them to hold their ground, but when they saw the flood coming in along with the enemy, they decided it was time not to listen to their commanders but to turn and run away as fast as possible.

> **Take ye the spoil of silver, take the spoil of gold: for there is none end of the store and glory out of all the pleasant furniture [Nah. 2:9].**

"Take ye the spoil of silver, take the spoil of gold." The enemy is invited to take the spoil of silver and to take the spoil of gold. "For there is none end of the store and glory out of all the pleasant furniture." The city of Nineveh was very wealthy and highly ornate. The palaces were beautiful, and the people lived in luxury because of the success they had had in warfare. You see, the Assyrians had brought in booty from all of the great nations of that day—even the southern kingdom of Judah was paying tribute to them at that time—so that the city had become very wealthy.

> **She is empty, and void, and waste: and the heart melteth, and the knees smite together, and much pain is in all loins, and the faces of them all gather blackness [Nah. 2:10].**

"She is empty, and void, and waste." Assyria had brought in booty from everywhere else and had gathered it all in one place, but their enemies came in and took it all out.

"And the heart melteth, and the knees smite together." When your knees smite together, it means that you are afraid, it means there is fear in your heart. This is what happened to the Assyrians.

"And much pain is in all loins, and the faces of them all gather blackness." This was a time of great fear and dread because the Assyrians knew that they were hated by the world of that day. All their neighbors hated them because of their brutality. Now vengeance was being taken out upon them. Instead of the blood being all drawn from their faces, Nahum says that "the faces of them all gather blackness." I take it that this means that they were putting on sackcloth and throwing ashes upon their heads.

> **Where is the dwelling of the loins, and the feedingplace of the young lions, where the lion, even the old lion, walked, and the lion's whelp, and none made them afraid? [Nah. 2:11].**

Both Assyria and Babylon used the lion as the symbol of their empires. Nahum could be referring here to the actual lions which the Assyrians had there, or he could be referring to their strong young men because the lion was the symbol of the strength of the kingdom. The whole point is that, whether it is the literal lions or the strength of their army, they are gone—they've left, or they've been killed.

> **The lion did tear in pieces enough for his whelps, and strangled for his lionesses, and filled his holes with prey, and his dens with ravin [Nah. 2:12].**

Whether these were the literal lions or the Assyrian army, they had once been well-fed, but now all of that is ended. They no longer have anything to eat because all has been taken away by the enemy.

Behold, I am against thee, saith the LORD of hosts, and I will burn her chariots in the smoke, and the sword shall devour thy young lions: and I will cut off thy prey from the earth, and the voice of thy messengers shall no more be heard [Nah. 2:13].

"Behold, I am against thee, saith the LORD of hosts." God doesn't say that very often. He says it only here and to Gog and Magog in Ezekiel 38 and 39. Many of us believe that the reference in Ezekiel is directed to modern Russia. That is pretty much established today by conservative scholarship. No one but a liberal who disregards facts and evidence would say that that passage does not refer to modern Russia. God says there to Russia, "I am against you," and He sets down a pattern for us. Russia has had the gospel; actually, they had it before we did. But today communism is opposed to God. It is atheistic; its basic philosophy is that it is opposed to God. But God beat them to the draw. He said to them long before they appeared as a nation, "I am against you."

Here in Nahum He also says, "I am against you," and He is talking to Nineveh. They were a people who had had a personal messenger from God (Jonah), and they had turned to the living God, but now they have turned from Him. When you have had the light and you reject it, the Lord Jesus put it like this: ". . . If therefore the light that is in thee be darkness, how great is that darkness!" (Matt. 6:23). In other words, if the light is shining right into your eyes and you say you cannot see, that means you are blind. This reminds me of the story of a young man who was in a mine explosion together with other men. The rescuers got to them as quickly as they could, taking away all of the wreckage and debris between those on the outside and the trapped miners. When they got through to them, the first thing they did was to turn on a light. But this young man stood there after the light came on and said, "Why don't they turn on the light?" Everybody looked at him in amazement because they knew then that the explosion had blinded him. But, you see, as long as they were in darkness, nobody could tell that he was blind. He couldn't tell it himself because he thought the lights were still out. "If therefore the light that is in thee be darkness,

how great is that darkness!"—it means you are blind. This is the picture that Nahum gives to us. The Assyrians had had light, but they
rejected it; and when you reject light, your responsibility is greater.

"I will burn her chariots in the smoke, and the sword shall devour
thy young lions." Again, this could be literal lions or the young men,
but I believe it refers to their young men because the lion was the symbol of the strength of the nation.

"And I will cut off thy prey from the earth, and the voice of thy
messengers shall no more be heard." This is a note of finality. One
hundred years earlier God had graciously saved Nineveh when they
repented and turned to Him; but time has marched on, they have
lapsed into an awful apostasy, and God is now going to judge them.
He says to them, "I'm against you. I'm going to bring you down. I will
annihilate you, and you will never appear again." This ought to be a
message today to those who have completely turned their backs upon
God: it means total judgment.

CHAPTER 3

In chapter 3 Nahum gives the cause for and justifies God's destruction of the city of Nineveh. Nineveh's destruction is an example of the fact that ". . . whatsoever a man soweth, that shall he also reap" (Gal. 6:7). This is also true of a nation. You will find that in many ways God deals with individuals and nations in a very similar manner.

Many literary critics have found in this third chapter one of the most vivid descriptions of the destruction of a city that is imaginable. You will not find anything in any language more descriptive than this.

> **Woe to the bloody city! it is all full of lies and robbery; the prey departeth not [Nah. 3:1].**

We are given here a picture of the internal condition of the city of Nineveh. "Woe to the bloody city!" Nineveh, as the capital of Assyria, was known in the ancient world to be very brutal, very bloody. They were feared and dreaded by other nations. The army of the Assyrians, although it actually moved rather slowly, was just like a hurricane which devours everything in its pathway. As I mentioned before, at times an entire community would commit suicide rather than suffer the brutal attack of Assyria.

"It is all full of lies." Assyria was a nation which could never be depended upon. She was not faithful to fulfill the promises which she made to other nations to help them and protect them.

What better description could you have even of our own country right now? I feel that we are given very few facts but a great deal of propaganda today. This is true not only of Washington, D.C., and the news media but of all areas of our society. This is true of our government regardless of which party the information comes from. My opinion of our two-party system is that what we have is Tweedledum and Tweedledee—you can pick either one of them. At one point in my life I thought I needed to change from one party to the other, and I did change. But now I need another change, not back to where I came from but to be free of this whole thing in which I am fed nothing in the world but propaganda and never given the truth. The one thing that is needed today is the truth.

One of the reasons God judged the city of Nineveh was that it was "all full of lies and robbery." These things characterized the life of the city. Likewise, our homes today are not safe. I was recently in the home of friends in Louisville, Kentucky. They are lovely folk, and they have a very lovely southern home in which they have some beautiful antiques. Do you know that they have had to put bars on their windows and double and triple locks on their doors! Where do you think we live today? We say that we live in a nation of law and order—but it hasn't been that. What an apt description this verse is of the United States! When I first began to study this, I felt like asking Nahum, "Are you talking about us? You're giving a vivid description of Nineveh, but it is also a picture of my own nation."

The Books of Jonah and Nahum reveal that God deals with gentile nations and that He did so back in the days of the Old Testament. They also show that the government of God moves in the governments of men. God today will overrule the sin of man. He will overrule a nation. As you come down through history, you see great civilizations, one after another, crumbling in the dust and the debris of the ages. Why? Because God judged them, friend—that is the reason why. The United States is no pet of God. We're not something special. We think we are. We can boast of the fact that right now we are the strongest nation in the world, but even that might be questionable today. We live in a security that may be a false security, because God brings great nations down, and He makes that very clear here.

The noise of a whip, and the noise of the rattling of the wheels, and of the prancing horses, and of the jumping chariots [Nah. 3:2].

Nahum gives a graphic description of these chariots. They are like armored tanks—they were the tanks of the ancient world. As they came inside the city, you could hear the noise of the whip as the driver whipped up his horse. You could hear the rattling of the wheels and the noise "of the prancing horses, and of the jumping [bounding] chariots." The chariots were leaping over everything, especially dead bodies.

The first two verses of this chapter describe the internal condition of Ninevah. Lies and robbery marked the culture and the climate of the city. This is the reason they acted as they did on the outside toward their enemies—their brutality, their total unconcern for other nations, their lording it over others. The very cause for their methods is that *internally* they were wrong. You see, man does not become a sinner because he sins. He sins because he *is* a sinner. Fundamentally, on the inside, man is a sinner, and that accounts for his actions. I am sure that many people in that day said of the Assyrians, "These people are uncivilized!" Inside the city, it was full of lies and robbery. That which did not characterize our nation years ago (there was a great deal of it, but it wasn't the predominant thing)—lies and robbery—just happens to characterize the internal condition of our nation today. Why? Because we are highly civilized? No. It is because we are sinners. My friend, we are sinners.

The horseman lifteth up both the bright sword and the glittering spear: and there is a multitude of slain, and a great number of carcases; and there is none end of their corpses; they stumble upon their corpses [Nah. 3:3].

The number of the dead was unbelievable. I tell you, if a well-placed bomb were dropped somewhere in this country, we would probably see the same sort of thing. There are nations who may pretend to be friendly but who would not hesitate for five seconds to drop that bomb on this country if they thought they could get by with it. And I'm beginning to think that they believe they can get by with it.

We have in verses 3–4 that which characterized the external conditions of Nineveh. They had been a brutal and cruel enemy, and they were now reaping what they had sown.

Because of the multitude of the whoredoms of the wellfavoured harlot, the mistress of witchcrafts, that selleth nations through her whoredoms, and families through her witchcrafts [Nah. 3:4].

"Because of the multitude of the whoredoms of the wellfavoured harlot." The city of Nineveh is here likened unto a harlot. She was the one whom all the nations played up to. Note the shame of this city. God likens her to a harlot, a "wellfavoured harlot," suggesting that all the world courted her.

"The mistress of witchcrafts, that selleth nations through her whoredoms, and families through her witchcrafts." Witchcraft is mentioned twice here. This is a reference to the occult. Don't for one moment think that the idolatry of the ancient world was meaningless. The apostle Paul called an idol ". . . nothing in the world . . ." (1 Cor. 8:4), but back of the idol is Satan, and back of idolatry is that which is satanic. I do not need to labor this point today. If you are not acquainted with what is happening today in the world of the occult, then you have not been to Southern California. It is not happening just among a bunch of down-and-outers or a bunch of criminals or in the underworld. The occult is active on our college campuses today and in the best sections of our cities. People are given over to witchcraft today. It is amazing how many people will buy their horoscope, which they will then follow. Many folk carry amulets, good luck pieces, charms, little dolls, and all that sort of thing. This is growing by leaps and bounds in a materialistic age and culture, which thought it had graduated from such things, but now we find there has been a return to it. This is exactly what the great city of Nineveh had turned to, and God says that He is justified in judging the city because of its harlotry and witchcraft.

The Book of Revelation tells us that when we come to the end of this age, the organized church will become a harlot, engaging in this type of thing. I am of the opinion that we can see a movement in that direction even now. All of this is very dangerous today. I know a very fine Pentecostal preacher who preaches the Word of God and believes in speaking in tongues and in healing. He expressed to me that there is a real danger in the tongues movement. He said, "Not only does our group speak in tongues, there are those today in the occult who are also doing it. In my own church, we are being very careful about this sort of thing." This man is a spiritually enlightened man, and he is rather reluctant to engage in "tongues" speaking. I would put up a warning to you today, friend: just because a thing seems to have a mark of the supernatural on it does not mean it is scriptural. You had better examine it very carefully to see whether it is scriptural. If it is supernatural and not scriptural, it is not of God. And there is only one other fellow who is in the business of the supernatural other than God, and that is Satan. Satan will ape God and imitate Him in every way that he possibly can.

God is giving to us the reason He judged Nineveh. He is justifying His actions in destroying this city. Now He makes this very remarkable statement—

> **Behold I am against thee, saith the Lord of hosts; and I will discover thy skirts upon thy face, and I will shew the nations thy nakedness, and the kingdoms thy shame [Nah. 3:5].**

"Behold, I am against thee, saith the Lord of hosts." This is the second time that God says this to Nineveh. He also says this to Gog and Magog in Ezekiel 38—39. We believe that definitely refers to Russia. When I graduated from seminary, I would not accept that Ezekiel 38—39 referred to Russia. So I decided to make a study of it on my own, and I now have several reasons why I am confident that it is Russia which is mentioned there. Russia is a nation which wasn't even in existence in Ezekiel's day, but God said to them, "I am against you." Well, we now know why He said that—they are an atheistic nation.

Assyria was a nation to whom God said, "I am against you," not because they were atheistic but because they were polytheistic. Assyria was given over to idolatry—back of the idol was the occult, back of the idol was witchcraft. Witchcraft has become a reality to many today. Men are finding that there is a reality to it. And it is those in the upper echelon who are making this discovery. I have been told on rather good authority, from those who are in our capital of Washington, that it is amazing and alarming to see the number of people there who appeal to fortune-tellers and to horoscopes in an attempt to interpret the future. Men want to know the future. But God said to Nineveh, a city greatly involved in the occult, "I am against thee."

"I will discover thy skirts upon thy face." In other words, "I am going to uncover thy skirts from thy face." We live in a day of a great deal of nudity. With their tongues in their cheeks, men try to call it art to present that which is salacious and sinful and suggestive. There is a great display of the nude by both men and women today. The Assyrian civilization had sunk pretty low but not as low as we have. They did not display the human body—they were not given over to that. It was a *disgrace* for a woman to be displayed nude. God speaks here of the shame that He is going to bring upon Nineveh. He says, "I will uncover thy skirts from thy face. I am going to pull your skirts up over your face. You have been a harlot, and I'm going to reveal you and all of the lurid details." Believe me, that was a real disgrace for them.

"I will shew the nations thy nakedness, and the kingdoms thy shame." That is what God said He would do to this nation. Assyria went down, my friend. A great nation, a great civilization, with all its riches and power, went down into the dust never to rise again. God said that is what He would do to them.

> **And I will cast abominable filth upon thee, and will make thee vile, and will set thee as a gazingstock [Nah. 3:6].**

God says to Ninevah through Nahum, "I am going to bring you down. I'm opposed to you. I will expose you to the world for what you are." The excavations which have brought to light this great civilization reveal that all of this is quite accurate. And the Book of Nahum just happens to be a vivid prophecy which was given long before this actually took place. This is something quite amazing, is it not?

All of this description which is given here is something I do not want to pass over lightly because it has such a tremendous application for us today and is such an apt picture of the present day. The Book of Nahum reveals God's method in dealing with the nations of the world. I do not think He has changed His method, and if He hasn't, we are in trouble, and I mean deep trouble, my friend. We ought to be praying for our nation.

God calls this city a harlot, saying that He is absolutely going to display all of the shame and filth and vileness of this great civilization and make it a gazingstock, a spectacle, to the world. Such was the end of the great Assyrian Empire.

And it shall come to pass, that all they that look upon thee shall flee from thee, and say, Nineveh is laid waste: who will bemoan her? whence shall I seek comforters for thee? [Nah. 3:7].

In other words, God says, "Where in the world will I get people to come and mourn over this city? Nobody will mourn over it. Nobody will weep over it. There will be no mourners there." That is a very sad situation, a very sad one indeed. Several funeral home directors here in Pasadena became my personal friends over the years and would sometimes call me to conduct a funeral. One of the saddest experiences that I ever had was the funeral I conducted for a dear old man. He was a Christian who had come out here from the east with his wife for the sake of her health. She had died, and then he became bedridden, and people forgot about him. When he died, I guess many didn't even recognize his name. When I went down to conduct the funeral, there wasn't anybody there. Nobody came—to me it was the saddest thing. I knew the funeral director pretty well, and I went to him and said, "Get all your office workers and come on in there. We're going to have a funeral service." He rounded up everyone that he could and brought them in. We had about a dozen folk. So I brought a gospel message, a message of hope for the Christian. It was wonderful to be able to say, "Jesus died for our sins, and He rose again for our justification." But it was sad to have a funeral service like that, where no friends attended. God said that there were not going to be any mourners at the funeral of Nineveh. Nahum prophesied that the whole world would rejoice in that day, and they did. When God said this through Nahum, no one would have believed it unless he had believed God and accepted it by faith, but it came to pass just as God said it would.

> **Art thou better than populous No, that was situate among the rivers, that has the waters round about it, whose rampart was the sea, and her wall was from the sea? [Nah. 3:8].**

"Art thou better than populous No?"—No-Amon was what we know as Thebes, the great capital of upper Egypt. Dr. Charles Feinberg's books on the minor prophets are very excellent—I know of none better. I would like to quote from his book, *Jonah, Micah and Nahum* (p. 147), in which he describes the city of No-Amon:

> It was the capital city of the Pharaohs of the Eighteenth to the Twentieth Dynasties, and boasted such architecture as the Greeks and Romans admired. The Greeks called it Diospolis, because the Egyptian counterpart of Jupiter was worshipped there. It was located on both banks of the river Nile. On the eastern bank were the famous temples at Karnak and Luxor. Homer, the first Greek poet, spoke of it as having 100 gates. Its ruins cover an area of some 27 miles. Amon, the chief god of the Egyptians, was shown on Egyptian relics as a figure with a human body and a ram's head. The judgment of this godless and idolatrous city was foretold by Jeremiah (46:25) and Ezekiel (30:14–16). No-Amon was situated favorably among the canals of the Nile with the Nile itself as a protection. The Nile appears as a sea when it overflows its banks annually. Nineveh can read her fate in that of No-Amon, for she is no better than the mighty Egyptian capital.

God is saying to Nineveh that the city of Thebes should have been an example to the Assyrian Empire. The Assyrians were the ones who had destroyed Thebes, a great city which had seemed impregnable. It seemed that no one could take it, but the Assyrians did take it and destroy it. This should have been an example to the Assyrians. God had judged Thebes, and He is here justifying the fact that He will also judge Nineveh. The government of God moves in the governments of men in this world today.

"Art thou better than populous No, that was situate among the rivers. . . ." "Rivers" is used in the plural to mean a great deal of water. When the Nile River would overflow at the flood season, it looked like the ocean. ". . . That had the waters round about it, whose rampart was the sea, and her wall was from the sea?" Thebes was built so that at the flood season it would not be flooded at all. Rather, the water provided a natural protection for the city.

Ethiopia and Egypt were her strength, and it was infinite; Put and Lubim were thy helpers [Nah. 3:9].

These were the allies of Thebes which were located around her. The city of Thebes, at one time the capital of the Egyptian Empire, felt that it could never fall because there was a big desert on both sides, the Nile River was a protection, and they had allies to the north and to the south. How could anybody get to them? But the Assyrians did. The Assyrians, in turn, felt that they were impregnable in their day. And today we feel that we have enough atomic weapons and other sophisticated hardware to defend ourselves. My friend, when God's time comes, we will go down. Our best defense today simply does not happen to be in the area of military weapons. Our best defense would be a return to God and to a recognition of Him in our government. I am not impressed by what I see in Washington. They have a little prayer breakfast and then, I'm told, some of them step outside and cuss up a storm! Some men make a profession of being Christians, and yet their language is so vile you cannot even listen to it. What hypocrisy there is today! Is God going to let us off? Are we something special? I think not. Our best defense today would be once again to have men of character in government—even if they were not Christians, if they would at least espouse the great morality set forth in the Word of God. That is the thing that built our nation. I am not greatly impressed with some of our founding fathers. I do not think, for example, that Thomas Jefferson was a Christian, but I will say that he had a respect for the Word of God. He believed in the morality of the Word of God. When we despise and contradict that morality as we do today, God cannot bless us as a nation, and I do not think He will.

> **Yet was she carried away, she went into captivity: her young children also were dashed in pieces at the top of all the streets: and they cast lots for her honourable men, and all her great men were bound in chains [Nah. 3:10].**

This is what Assyria had done to Thebes, and now chickens are coming home to roost. "Be not deceived; God is not mocked: for whatsoever a man soweth, that shall he also reap" (Gal. 6:7).

> **Thou also shalt be drunken: thou shalt be hid, thou also shalt seek strength because of the enemy [Nah. 3:11].**

The Assyrians will try to fortify their courage by getting drunk, but that is not going to help them a bit.

> **All thy strong holds shall be like fig trees with the first-ripe figs: if they be shaken, they shall even fall into the mouth of the eater [Nah. 3:12].**

I used to have a fig tree in my yard. When the figs were ripe, all you had to do was just touch a branch, and they all would come tumbling down. This is what Nahum says to Nineveh here: "All your defenses are like that. The minute the enemy comes, he is going to break right through them."

> **Behold, thy people in the midst of thee are women: the gates of thy land shall be set wide open unto thine enemies: the fire shall devour thy bars [Nah. 3:13].**

I believe that the thought here is that the men were acting like women. The men were very womanly. Or this could mean that women were actually the ones in the positions of authority. Frankly, I do not think God is for the women's liberation movement which we have today. I still believe that woman's place is in the home. I feel very frankly that the church is at fault in using women in too many offices in the church. A woman's first place is not to teach a Sunday school class. She is to raise her own family—that is her place. Women are being taken away from their homes by church work and every other kind of work. Unless she is forced to work for a living because her husband has passed on or is unable to work, I do not believe a woman's working is justified. I know that I will get reactions for saying this, but I am saying it because I think that this is one mark of the disintegration and downfall of civilization.

> **Draw thee waters for the siege, fortify thy strong holds: go into clay, and tread the mortar, make strong the brickkiln [Nah. 3:14].**

At the last minute, the Assyrians would get busy making bricks to fortify themselves. They would heat up water, which they would carry to the top of the city wall. They would then pour a bucket of the scalding water down upon the fellow who was scaling the wall. He was through scaling the wall, I can assure you of that—he would soon find himself back on the ground.

> **There shall the fire devour thee; the sword shall cut thee off, it shall eat thee up like the cankerworm: make thyself many as the cankerworm, make thyself many as the locusts [Nah. 3:15].**

Nahum prophesies that they will try to bring in reinforcements but that they will not help.

> **Thou hast multiplied thy merchants above the stars of heaven: the cankerworm spoileth, and flieth away [Nah. 3:16].**

Each year their national wealth increased, for they were great merchants, but all of that was going to come to an end.

> **Thy crowned are as the locusts, and thy captains as the great grasshoppers, which camp in the hedges in the cold day, but when the sun ariseth they flee away, and their place is not known where they are [Nah. 3:17].**

When the time came, the leaders would manage to escape, that is, for a little while anyway.

> **Thy shepherds slumber, O king of Assyria: thy nobles shall dwell in the dust: thy people is scattered upon the mountains, and no man gathereth them [Nah. 3:18].**

The leadership of Assyria disintegrated to the place where they no longer attempted to lead the nation.

I trust that I will not be misunderstood because I am not discussing politics, certainly not from any party viewpoint. (As far as I am concerned, I am disgusted with both of the major political parties in this nation of ours.) I believe that one of the great evidences of our disintegration and deterioration as a nation is the lack of leadership that exists on the national level, the state level, the county level, and even at the city and community levels. There is a lack of real leadership at all levels. It seems that the one with the big mouth and the big talk is the one who is elected. And it seems that the rich man is the one elected. Abraham Lincoln could not run for the office of President today—he wouldn't have enough money. God says that the lack of leadership, along with the other things He has mentioned, is what brought Assyria down.

What God has said in this chapter concerning Assyria fits our nation like a glove. One glove fits Assyria—and that's been fulfilled. The other glove fits the United States. But are we listening to God today? No. No one to speak of is paying any attention. Certainly the leadership of our nation is not. The tragedy of the hour is our retreat from God and our rejection of Jesus Christ, the Prince of Peace, the Savior of the world.

Listen to God's final words to Ninevah. He says this with a note of finality and of dogmatism. This makes your spine tingle. It is frightening indeed—

> **There is no healing of thy bruise; thy wound is grievous: all that hear the bruit of thee shall clap the hands over thee: for upon whom hath not thy wickedness passed continually? [Nah. 3:19].**

The Assyrian people had sinned and sinned and sinned—it was a way of life with them. When people want to point a finger and say that God is wrong, that God permits evil and does nothing about evil, God says to them, "I *do* do something about it." My friend, you can look around today at the many injustices in our world, but God *is* doing something about them. God is just and righteous. He was a God of love even when He destroyed Nineveh and wiped it clean like a dish. It disappeared off the face of the map and off the face of the earth—and God took full responsibility for its judgment.

(For Bibliography to Nahum, see Bibliography at the end of Habakkuk.)

HABAKKUK

The Book of
HABAKKUK

INTRODUCTION

Nahum, Habakkuk, and Zephaniah have a great deal in common. Each one gives a different facet of the dealings of God with mankind. They show how the government of God is integrated into the government of men. They also show God's dealings with the individual.

Another similarity is the fact that they come from approximately the same time period. In fact, they all could have been contemporaries, and the possibility is that they were. (It is difficult to nail down the specific dates of the prophets—and of many of the other Old Testament books. The reason, of course, is that the exact dates are not important.) At least we know that all three prophets fit into the period between the reigns of kings Josiah and Jehoiakim, which would also be the time of the prophet Jeremiah. The northern kingdom had already gone into captivity, and the southern kingdom was right on the verge of captivity. After Josiah, every king in the southern kingdom was a bad king. Nahum, Habakkuk, and Zephaniah all fit into that period of decline.

Although there are similarities, these books also differ from each other. Nahum dealt only with Nineveh, the capital of the Assyrian Empire. Nahum showed that God is just, righteous, and a God of love; yet He was absolutely right in judging that city.

Habakkuk approaches the problem from a little different viewpoint. He is a man with questions. He is disturbed about God's seeming indifference to the inquity of His own people. Habakkuk asks God, "Why don't You *do* something?" In our day a great many folk feel as Habakkuk did. They are asking, "Why doesn't God *do* something? Why doesn't He move into the affairs of men and stop the violence and injustice and suffering?"

God answered the question for Habakkuk by informing him that He was preparing a nation, Babylon, to punish Judah and to take her into captivity—unless she changed her ways. Well, if you think Habakkuk had a problem before, you can see that he really had a problem then! Habakkuk asked, "Why will You use Babylon—a nation that is definitely more wicked, more pagan, and more given over to idolatry than Your own people—to punish Judah?" God reveals to Habakkuk that He was not through with Babylon but would judge her also. This is God's method.

This book is very important in its relationship to the New Testament. It is generally conceded that the three great doctrinal books of the New Testament are Romans, Galatians, and Hebrews, all of which quote from Habakkuk. In fact, Habakkuk 2:4 is the background of their message: "The just shall live by his faith." So this little book looms upon the horizon of Scripture as being important. Don't let the brevity of it deceive you. Importance is not determined by *how much* you say but by *what* you say.

The name *Habakkuk* means "to embrace." Dr. Charles Feinberg (*Habakkuk, Zephaniah, Haggai*, p. 11) described Martin Luther's striking definition of this name:

> Habakkuk signifies an embracer, or one who embraces another, takes him into his arms. He embraces his people, and takes them to his arms, i.e., he comforts them and holds them up, as one embraces a weeping child, to quiet it with the assurance that, if God wills, it shall soon be better.

Habakkuk told us nothing of his personal life, even of the era in which he lived. I call him the doubting Thomas of the Old Testament because he had a question mark for a brain. His book is really unusual. It is not a prophecy in the strict sense of the term. It is somewhat like the Book of Jonah in that Habakkuk told of his own experience with God—his questions to God and God's answers. We could say that Habakkuk was born in the objective case, in the pluperfect tense, in the subjunctive mood. We write over him a big question mark until, in the last chapter and especially in the final two or three verses, we can put down an exclamation point. This book is the personal experience of the prophet told in poetry, as Jonah's was told in prose.

Habakkuk was an interesting man, and he has written a lovely book with real literary excellence. The final chapter is actually a song of psalm of praise and adoration to God, a very beautiful piece of literature.

The closing statement in the book, "To the chief singer [musician] on my stringed instruments," reveals that this book is a song. That little note was put there for the director of the orchestra and the choir. The final chapter of the book is a psalm of beauty. In fact, the entire prophecy is a gem. It has been translated into a metric version by A. C. Gaebelein (*The Annotated Bible*, pp. 214–219). Delitzsch wrote, "His language is classical throughout, full of rare and select turns and words." Moorehouse wrote, "It is distinguished for its magnificent poetry."

This little book opens in gloom and closes in glory. It begins with a question mark and closes with an exclamation point. Habakkuk is a big WHY? Why God permits evil is a question that every thoughtful mind has faced. I think that this book is the answer to that question. Will God straighten out the injustice of the world? This book answers that question. Is God doing anything about the wrongs of the world? This book says that He is. In my opinion it is possible to reduce the doubt of Thomas in the New Testament, of Habakkuk in the Old Testament, and of modern man into the one word. *Why?* It is the fundamental question of the human race. When we reduce all questions to the lowest common denominator, we come to the basic question: Why?

You can see that the message of Habakkuk is almost the opposite of the message of Nahum. In the Book of Nahum God was moving in judgment, and the question was: How can God be a God of love and judge as He is doing? Here in Habakkuk it is just the opposite: Why doesn't God do something about the evil in the world?

The theme of Habakkuk is faith. He has been called the prophet of faith. The great statement of Habakkuk 2:4, "the just shall live by his faith," has been quoted three times in the New Testament: Romans 1:17; Galatians 3:11; and Hebrews 10:38.

OUTLINE

I. Perplexity of the Prophet, Chapter 1
A. First Problem of the Prophet, Chapter 1:1–4
Why does God permit evil?
B. God's Answer, Chapter 1:5–11
God was raising up Chaldeans to punish Judah (v. 6).
C. Second Problem of the Prophet (greater than first),
Chapter 1:12–17
*Why would God permit His people to be punished by a
nation more wicked than they? Why did He not destroy the
Chaldeans?*

II. Perception of the Prophet, Chapter 2
A. Practice of the Prophet, Chapter 2:1
He took the secret problem to the secret place.
B. Patience of the Prophet, Chapter 2:2–3
He waited for the vision.
C. Pageant for the Prophet, Chapter 2:4
*The great divide in humanity: One group, which is
crooked, is flowing toward destruction; the other group, by
faith, is moving toward God. This is inevitable.*
D. Parable to the Prophet, Chapter 2:5–20
*The application is self-evident from the vision. The
Chaldeans, in turn, would be destroyed. God was moving
among the nations.*

III. Pleasure of the Prophet, Chapter 3
A. Prayer of the Prophet, Chapter 3:1–2
*The prophet, who thought God was doing nothing about
evil, now asks Him to remember to be merciful. Was he
afraid that God was doing too much?*
B. Program of God, Chapter 3:3–17
*God rides majestically in His own chariot of salvation
(v. 8).*

C. Position of the Prophet, Chapter 3:18–19
   He will rejoice (v. 18). He has come from pain to pleasure.

CHAPTER 1

THEME: The perplexity of the prophet

The burden which Habakkuk the prophet did see [Hab. 1:1].

"The burden" means the judgment. Actually, this is not Habakkuk's question, but rather it is the Lord's answer. The answer of God is really the prophecy of the Book of Habakkuk. The Lord's answer is judgment which Habakkuk called, as did the other prophets, "the burden."

FIRST PROBLEM OF THE PROPHET

Habakkuk's first problem is this: Why does God permit evil?

O Lord, how long shall I cry, and thou wilt not hear! even cry out unto thee of violence and thou wilt not save! [Hab. 1:2].

"O Lord, how long shall I cry, and thou wilt not hear!" Habakkuk is telling God that He is refusing to answer his prayers. He cries out in a night of despair as he sees violence among his people. And God is doing nothing and saying nothing. This is the elegy of Habakkuk. As we shall see, the book concludes with a paean of praise and a note of joy.

My friend, if you have a question, my feeling is that you ought to take it to the Lord as Habakkuk did. If you are sincere, you will get an answer from God.

Why dost thou show me iniquity, and cause me to behold grievance? for spoiling and violence are before me: and there are that raise up strife and contention.

> **Therefore the law is slacked, and judgment doth never
> go forth: for the wicked doth compass about the righ-
> teous; therefore wrong judgment proceedeth [Hab.
> 1:3-4].**

Here is his big question: Why does God permit this evil to continue among His own people—the iniquity, the injustice, the strife, and contention?

This is both an old question and a new question. It is one which you could ask today. Let's look at it in detail.

Habakkuk, as I suggested in the Introduction, probably wrote sometime after the time of King Josiah, the last good king of the southern kingdom of Judah. After Josiah there was Jehoahaz, a bad one who didn't last more than three months; then Jehoiakim came along and reigned eleven years, and he was a bad one. It was a time of disintegration, deterioration, and degradation in the kingdom. There was a breaking down of the Mosaic Law, and the people were turning away from God. The question was: Why was God permitting this evil?

While I was in a Bible conference in the east several years ago, I talked with two young professors, one from Vanderbilt University and the other from Missouri. They both were Christians and brilliant young men. They told me that the the godless professors would use this method to try to destroy young people's faith in the integrity of the Word of God. They would begin like this: "You do not believe that a God of love would permit evil in the world, do you? Do you think a loving God, kind in heart, would permit suffering in the world?"

The enemy, you will recall, used that same method with Eve, as recorded in Genesis 3. He said something like this: "Do you mean to tell me that God does not want you to eat of that tree? Why? That tree has the most delicious fruit of any tree in the garden, and if you eat it, your eyes will be opened, and you will become like God. I can't believe that a good God would forbid your eating of that tree. I just can't understand it!" He was destroying, you see, her confidence in the goodness of God. That is always where the enemy starts.

Habakkuk's question fitted into the local situation of his day. People were getting by with sin, and God was seemingly doing nothing about it. His question was, Why doesn't God judge the wicked? Why does God permit evil men and women to prosper? And isn't that a good question in our day? I'm sure that many of God's people have asked, 'Why doesn't God judge the evil in our nation today? Why does He permit the rich to get richer? And why is it that the average person is having to bear the burden of taxation and inflation? Why doesn't God do something about it?" Is this your question?

That was the psalmist's question in Psalm 73:2–3: "But as for me, my feet were almost gone; my steps had well nigh slipped. For I was envious at the foolish, when I saw the prosperity of the wicked." As he looked around, he saw that the ones who were prospering were the *wicked!* It almost robbed him of his faith. Why wasn't God doing something about it?

The people of Judah apparently felt that they were God's little pets and that He would not punish them for their sins. Probably the first time they did something evil they were apprehensive, wondering if God would punish them. When He did nothing, they assumed that He hadn't noticed or didn't care. The writer of Ecclesiastes says in chapter 8 verse 11: "Because sentence against an evil work is not executed speedily, therefore the heart of the sons of men is fully set in them to do evil."

I can remember when I was a boy and swiped my first watermelon. It was in the summertime, and a storm was coming up. By the time I had pulled a watermelon off the vine and had started to the fence with it, there was a flash of lightning and a clap of thunder the like of which you can only have in southern Oklahoma! I thought the Lord was judging me right there and then for what I had done. But the day came when I discovered that it wasn't judgment from God and I could do that sort of thing without fear.

Human nature does not change. The sins which were committed undercover in the backyard are now done openly in the front yard. Does that change the fact that sin is wrong in the sight of God and that He is going to judge every sin? No, God has not changed His standards or His procedures. Even though His execution against an evil work is not performed speedily, His judgment is sure to come eventually.

In our day very few people believe in the judgment of God. They feel like Habakkuk did when he saw his nation getting worse and worse until sin was flagrant and God was doing nothing about it. Don't you feel that way about conditions as they are? Is God doing anything about it today? It doesn't look as if He is. He even let a group of theologians up in New England come up with the idea a few years ago that God was dead. What they actually meant was that there is no God and there has never been a God. What made them arrive at such a conclusion? It is because they don't see Him interfering in the affairs of men today. But isn't He interfering? Isn't God overruling in the affairs of mankind today? He permitted us to go through a period of affluence, and folk became careless—even God's people became careless. Now we are in such a state that we wonder how much longer we are going to survive as a nation.

Habakkuk was a man with a very tender heart, and he hated to see lawlessness abounding and going unpunished. He hated to see the innocent people being threatened and exploited and destroyed. He was asking, "God, why aren't you doing something about it?"

Well, God had an answer for him, and He has an answer for you if this is your question.

GOD'S ANSWER

Behold ye among the heathen, and regard, and wonder marvellously: for I will work a work in your days, which ye will not believe, though it be told you [Hab. 1:5].

"Behold ye among the heathen," or better, "Behold ye among the nations." God is challenging Habakkuk to open his eyes and look about him, to get a world view of what He is doing. One great crisis after another has taken place. The great Assyrian Empire in the north has been conquered, and Nineveh, its capital, has been destroyed. On the banks of the Euphrates River, a kingdom is arising which already has won a victory over Egypt at Carchemish. Nebuchadnezzar is the victor, and he is bringing Babylon to the fore as a world power. God is saying to Habakkuk, "Behold ye among the nations—you think I'm not doing anything? I am not sitting on the fifty-yard line watching this little world. I am very much involved." He is not involved to the extent that He is subject to it and has to make certain plays because they are forced upon Him. God is moving in a sovereign way in the universe. He *is* doing something about sin—"Behold ye among the heathen, and regard, and wonder marvellously."

"For I will work a work in your days, which ye will not believe, though it be told you." God is saying, "It is going to be difficult for you to believe it. Instead of doing nothing, I am doing a great deal." In fact, Habakkuk is going to ask God to slow down when he finds out what God is doing.

"For I will work a work in your days, which ye will not believe, though it be told you" is quoted by Paul in the great sermon he gave in Antioch of Pisidia. (I have always felt that this is one of the greatest sermons Paul preached, and yet it is receiving very little attention in our day.) It is recorded in Acts 13. Now notice these words: "Be it known unto you therefore, men and brethren, that through this man [the Lord Jesus Christ] is preached unto you the forgiveness of sins: and by him all that believe are justified from all things, from which ye could not be justified by the law of Moses. Beware therefore, lest that come upon you, which is spoken of in the prophets; behold, ye despisers, and wonder, and perish: for I work a work in your days, a work which ye shall in no wise believe, though a man declare it unto you" (Acts 13:38–41). As you can see, Paul is quoting from Habakkuk 1:5. It is an amazing application of this verse. Paul is saying that God has provided a salvation, and He didn't do it (as Paul said elsewhere) in a corner. At the time of the Crucifixion, Jews from all over the world were in Jerusalem to celebrate the Passover. They carried the word everywhere that Jesus of Nazareth had died on a cross, and it was rumored that He was raised from the dead. Also, Jews from all over the world were back in Jerusalem for the celebration of Pentecost when the Holy Spirit came upon the little group of believers. Multitudes were saved at that time and in succeeding days. When that news went out, the Roman world ignored it at first. Paul is telling them that God has worked a work in their days, "a work which ye shall in no wise believe, though a man declare it unto you."

Today the world asks, "Why doesn't God do something about

sin?" My friend, God *has* done something about it! Over nineteen hundred years ago He gave His Son to die. He intruded into the affairs of the world. And He says that He is going to intrude *again* in the affairs of the world—yet today the world goes merrily along picking daisies and having a good time in sin. But God is moving. It is marvelous how Paul used Habakkuk 1:5.

And in Habakkuk's day God was moving. In spite of the lawlessness, the war, and the sin in all the nations, God was overruling and moving in judgment.

Now God is specific in what He was doing—

For, lo, I raise up the Chaldeans, that bitter and hasty nation, which shall march through the breadth of the land, to possess the dwellingplaces that are not theirs [Hab. 1:6].

God is saying to Habakkuk, 'Look around you. Down there on the banks of the Euphrates River, a nation is rising which will become the first great world power." (We can check with Daniel on that because Babylon is the head of gold, and it is the lion of Daniel's visions.) Babylon was number one on the parade of the great nations of the world.

"To possess the dwellingplaces that are not theirs." God is telling Habakkuk that the Babylonians are going to take the land of Judah away from them. It was a shock to Habakkuk to hear this.

A "bitter and hasty nation" is a good description of the Babylonian Empire. They were bitter, hateful, and hotheaded, marching for world conquest. They actually took the city of Jerusalem three times, and the third time they burned it to the ground. The Babylonians were a law unto themselves. They considered themselves the superior race, the dominant race, and did not recognize anyone as being equal to them.

They are terrible and dreadful: their judgment and their dignity shall proceed of themselves [Hab. 1:7].

"Their dignity shall proceed of themselves"—that is, they rely upon themselves. They have great self-confidence and are great boasters. These qualities are evident in Nebuchadnezzar, the founder of this great empire. In the Book of Daniel we find that Nebuchadnezzar suffered from a form of insanity, egomania, called hysteria by modern psychiatry. It was sort of a manic-depressive psychosis. The time came when he didn't even know who he was. In fact, he went out and ate grass like an animal.

> **Their horses also are swifter than the leopards, and are more fierce than the evening wolves: and their horsemen shall spread themselves, and their horsemen shall come from far; they shall fly as the eagle that hasteth to eat [Hab. 1:8].**

What a picture this is! The Babylonians used the cavalry as probably no other nation has used it. The Egyptians used chariots, and the Assyrians had the latest model in chariots. Now the Babylonians have a different method, the cavalry.

"More fierce than the evening wolves." I remember the hungry wolves in west Texas when I was a boy. After the snow had fallen, my dad warned us to be careful when we went outside. If there were a pack of wolves, it would be necessary to shoot one of them. Then when the blood began to flow, the pack would turn on the wounded wolf and devour him so that we could escape.

"They shall fly as the eagle that hasteth to eat." The Babylonian army would come like hungry animals and ferocious birds and seize upon their prey. That was the story of the Chaldeans, the Babylonians.

> **They shall come all for violence: their faces shall sup up as the east wind, and they shall gather the captivity as the sand [Hab. 1:9].**

"They shall come all for violence." God's people had been engaging in violence, but they hadn't seen anything yet. Wait until the Babylonians get there. God is going to give them a good dose of violence! You see, chickens do come home to roost—". . . whatsoever a man soweth, that shall he also reap" (Gal. 6:7).

"Their faces shall sup up as the east wind" has also been translated as "the set of their faces is forward." In both translations the thought seems to be that the enemy will be formidable and irresistible in its advance.

"And they shall gather the captivity as the sand." Nebuchadnezzar led his forces against Jerusalem three times. At the final attack, he burned the city and also the temple and took the survivors into captivity. The Babylonians had only one purpose in view, which was to capture as many nations and as many peoples as possible and make slaves of them. This is what happened to the southern kingdom of Judah.

> **And they shall scoff at the kings, and the princes shall be a scorn unto them: they shall deride every strong hold; for they shall heap dust, and take it [Hab. 1:10].**

"And they shall scoff at the kings, and the princes shall be a scorn unto them." They were confident in their own strength and in the power of their heathen gods. As the Assyrians before them, they were arrogant as they marched through the earth.

"They shall deride every strong hold; for they shall heap dust, and take it." They had only to cast up bulwarks to capture walled cities; and, when the cities surrendered, they took the inhabitants into captivity.

> **Then shall his mind change, and he shall pass over, and offend, imputing this his power unto his god [Hab. 1:11].**

This is exactly what Nebuchadnezzar did. In Daniel 4:30 we read the words of this man: "The king spake, and said, Is not this great Babylon, that I have built for the house of the kingdom by the might of my power, and for the honor of my majesty?" He was lifted up with pride. He was an egomaniac. He trusted completely in himself with no trust in God. And we have a few of those around today—trusting in self rather than in God. In my own nation there is a lack of humility. And, as in Nebuchadnezzar, it is a form of insanity. Each political party— not one, but all of them—boasts about what it can do or has done. They point the finger of guilt at the other party and at those holding office. Well, I agree they should repent, but my feeling is that everyone who is at the other end of the pointing fingers should also repent. Our big problem in America is that we depend upon our own strength, our own power, and our own ability. I turn off certain television programs because I am tired of listening to individuals boasting of their accomplishments, which are not very much. It reminds me of that scriptural suggestion of a mountain travailing. What did it bring forth? Another mountain? No, it brought forth a mouse! Although the boasting of great men today sounds like a mountain, what they have accomplished is about as big as a mouse.

In these verses God is saying to Habakkuk, "You think I am doing nothing about the sin of My people, but I am preparing a nation down yonder on the banks of the Euphrates River, and if My people do not repent, I'm going to turn the Babylonians loose." My friend, they came, and the record indicates that their destruction of Jerusalem was fierce and terrible. Some of the things they did when they took the people of Judah captive were almost unspeakable.

SECOND PROBLEM OF THE PROPHET

Now when God says that He is going to use the Babylonians to judge His people, this raises another question in Habakkuk's mind. If you think he had a question before, he *really has a question now*.

> **Art thou not from everlasting, O LORD my God, mine Holy One? We shall not die. O LORD, thou hast ordained them for judgment; and, O mighty God, thou hast established them for correction [Hab. 1:12].**

This was Habakkuk's problem: Since the Babylonians were even more wicked than the people of Judah, why would God choose a more wicked nation to punish a nation which was comparatively less wicked? This would not be the first time God had used such a method. In Isaiah 10:5 the Assyrian is called the rod of God's anger. In other words, God used Assyria like a whip in order to chastise the northern kingdom. After God had used Assyria for the chastisement of Israel, He judged Assyria for her own sins.

We find the same thing repeated here. God is going to use a wicked nation, Babylon, to chastise His people. When He is through with that chastisement, He will judge Babylon. God did just that. He moves in the affairs of men.

But the problem remains: How can a holy God use a sinful nation to accomplish His purposes?

This may be a new thought for you. You probably have heard it said—even from some pulpits—that God would never let Russia overcome the United States because we are the fair-haired boys, the good guys, the fine people. We are the ones who send missionaries to godless nations. God would never use Russia to chastise us. My friend, if you believe the Bible, you will see that God's method is to use a sinful nation to judge a people who are less sinful. If we could see what God is doing today behind the scenes, I am sure it would terrify us. I believe He is actually moving against our nation. Why? Because at one time our nation had a knowledge of God, superficial though it may have been. The Bible was once held in reverence. Very few people knew much about it, but it was respected. In our day the Bible is ignored and absolutely rejected by the nation. They may take an oath by placing their hand upon it, but they neither know nor care to know what is between its covers. Will God allow our nation to continue in its godlessness and in its flagrant sins? I don't think so. Will God use a godless nation to chastise us? Well, that was Habakkuk's question. Why would God, who is a holy God, use a pagan, heathen people to chastise His people?

Listen to Habakkuk's eloquent complaint. "Art thou not from everlasting, O LORD my God, mine Holy One?" God has come out of eternity; He is the *eternal* God. "O LORD my God, mine Holy

One"—Habakkuk says, in effect, "You are a Holy God. How can you use a nation like Babylon? Word has come to us that there is a great nation rising down there on the banks of the Euphrates River, but I never dreamed that You would use them against us! They have been friendly to us." When King Hezekiah was sick, they sent ambassadors to him, and he gave them the red-carpet treatment, showing them all the treasures of the kingdom. Of course, the ambassadors made note of that because they would be coming back one day to get that gold. But Habakkuk didn't realize all that. He never dreamed that God would use Babylon to chastise Judah. He didn't understand why a holy God would use such a method.

Then he says, "We shall not die." He was right about that. This goes back to the promises of God to Abraham, to Isaac, and to Jacob. God made promises to Moses and to Joshua and to David. He gave promises to the prophets who had appeared on the scene before Habakkuk. God had said that He would never let the nation perish. "We shall not die."

That is a good statement, by the way, to drop down upon our millennial friends who believe that God is through with the nation Israel. God is not through with them; God has an eternal purpose with them, just as He has with the church which He is calling out of this world. And, thank God, the child of God today can say, "We shall not die." The Lord Jesus Christ came to this earth to die—He said He did—to die in your stead and in my stead. He said, "I am the resurrection and the life," and He came back from the dead. He ". . . was delivered for our offences, and was raised again for our justification" (Rom. 4:25). The Lord Jesus said to the two weeping sisters of Lazarus, ". . . I am the resurrection, and the life: he that believeth in me, though he were *dead* [think of that!], yet shall he live." When Habakkuk said, "We shall not die," he was right; they wouldn't. "And whosoever liveth and believeth in me shall never die. Believest thou this?" (John 11:25–26, italics mine). This is the message of the gospel. It is something for you and me to believe. Of course, someday you are going to die physically, but are you dead now spiritually? If you are, you will be dead in trespasses and sins for the rest of eternity, and that means eternal separation from God. God is a holy God, and He is not going to take *sin* to heaven. But He has promised that if we will trust His Son, He will give us eternal life. God says, "If you will believe that you are a sinner, that you don't deserve salvation and can't work for it, then I offer it to you as a gift. And by My grace you will be saved. You will receive eternal life. He that hath the Son hath life." My friend, do you have the Son today? If you do, you have life, eternal life, and you will not die.

When Habakkuk said to God, "We shall not die," he was on the right track, but he just couldn't understand (as many of us can't understand) some of the performance of God in this world. God had told Habakkuk earlier that he needed to get a perspective of it. You and I have a tremendous advantage in our day because we have the perspective of history. We can look back to Habakkuk's day and even beyond to the very beginning of the human family. We have a very good perspective of God's dealing with the nations of this world and of God's dealing with the nation Israel. Also, God is dealing today with His church that is in the world.

God moves in a mysterious way His wonders to perform. He has told us that His ways are not our ways, that His thoughts are not our thoughts. "For my thoughts are not your thoughts, neither are your ways my ways, saith the LORD. For as the heavens are higher than the earth, so are my ways higher than your ways, and my thoughts than your thoughts" (Isa. 55:8–9).

My friend, do not be disturbed if you are not thinking as God thinks. You are not God. Unfortunately, many folk try to take His place. They are trying to work for their salvation, thinking that their character and their good works will merit them salvation. They expect God to pat them on the head someday and say, "You were certainly a nice, sweet little boy down there." Yet, actually, they were corrupt sinners, alienated from the life of God, with no capacity for God whatsoever. If you come to the Father, you will come His way, or you are not going to get there. We need to recognize this, my friend. We are a nation of proud people who need to be deflated as a pin deflates a balloon. Instead of blaming everyone else for the problems in our nation, or the problems in our church, or the problems in our home, we should fall on our knees before God and confess our own sins—"not my brother, nor my sister, but it's *me*, Oh, Lord, standin' in the need of prayer."

This was the condition of the nation of Judah in the days of Habakkuk. He said to God, "We shall not die."

"O LORD, thou hast ordained *them* for judgment." Here is Habakkuk pointing his finger at Babylon. "*They* are the bad guys, and we are the good guys." It is amazing how quickly we can change our point of view. For years I went out to Flagstaff, Arizona, to the Southwest Bible and Missionary Conference. I always enjoyed being out there with the opportunity it offered to have fellowship with the Indians. It was there I learned a good example of man's way of looking at things. One of the young Indian pastors said to me, "You know, Dr. McGee, in the old days when the Indians would raid a village and kill some of the whites, it was called a massacre. But when the whites raided an Indian village and destroyed *all* the Indians, it was called a victory." It is interesting how we always class ourselves with the good guys.

"O mighty God, thou hast established them for correction." In other words, Habakkuk is saying, "Lord, it really isn't us who are bad after all. They are the mean fellows. They are the ones You should judge and correct." Has he forgotten that he went to the Lord and asked the Lord why He wasn't doing something about the evil among His own people? Habakkuk had pointed out that the people were flaunting the law and were ignoring God, paying no attention to God's commands. Habakkuk had accused God of not doing anything about the situation. Has he forgotten that?

Now here is Habakkuk's argument—

> **Thou art of purer eyes than to behold evil, and canst not look on iniquity: wherefore lookest thou upon them that deal treacherously, and holdest thy tongue when the wicked devoureth the man that is more righteous than he? [Hab. 1:13].**

"Thou art of purer eyes than to behold evil, and canst not look on iniquity." That is a true statement. A holy God cannot look upon evil and iniquity. That is the reason no one can go to heaven with his sin on him. That is why we must all have the forgiveness for our sins. We all need the cleansing power of the blood of the Lamb. We must be given a new nature. We must be born again. Even Nicodemus, a very religious man, needed to be born again and to receive a new nature. Religion will not wash away sin. It is the blood of the Lord Jesus Christ who died and rose again that will wash away sin. God cannot look on iniquity, and He never will look on iniquity. That is why there is no entrance into heaven for you until your sin has been dealt with.

You see, when God forgives you, it is because the penalty for your sin has been paid for by His Son. God is not a sentimental old gentleman who doesn't have the heart to judge little man down here on this earth. God is a holy God who will not look upon iniquity. Your sin will have to be confessed and forgiven before you can be accepted by Him.

"Wherefore lookest thou upon them that deal treacherously." Habakkuk says, "You can't trust those Babylonians. They are sinners and a bunch of crooks!" He was right. They were. But God was going to use them to accomplish his purpose.

This is frightening to me. Don't ever get the idea that God cannot use a godless nation to chasten another nation. I speak now from the point of view of a white man and an American. For years the white man in all the great nations of Europe ruled the world through those great, proud nations. Then America became one of the leading nations of the world. God humiliated us in the war with Vietnam. He is humiliating us in our dealings with the Middle East. All they need to do is turn off the supply of oil, and suddenly we take a nosedive. God deals with the nations of the world in interesting ways. I watch what has been happening in the world with a great deal of interest. I have come to the conclusion that God is still moving among the nations of the world today. You and I may be frightened as we contemplate what lies ahead, but God is not frightened. He is still in charge. Nothing is out of His control. He is still running this universe.

"Wherefore lookest thou upon them that deal treacherously, and holdest thy tongue when the wicked devoureth the man that is more righteous than he?" Habakkuk said the wrong thing here. It is not "the man that is more righteous than he" because *none* are righteous. He should have said, "the man who is a greater sinner than he." But God didn't say that He was going to punish on that basis. God is going to use the Babylonians to punish His people.

This brings us to one of the most eloquent sections of the Word of God.

> **And makest men as the fishes of the sea, as the creeping things, that have no ruler over them?**
>
> **They take up all of them with the angle, they catch them in their net, and gather them in their drag: therefore they rejoice and are glad.**
>
> **Therefore they sacrifice unto their net, and burn incense unto their drag; because by them their portion is fat, and their meat plenteous [Hab. 1:14–16].**

"And makest men as the fishes of the sea, as the creeping things, that have no ruler over them" refers to the callousness with which the Babylonians handled their enemies, treating them as fish of the sea or as creeping things in the soil which have no defense.

The angle and the net and the drag represent the armies and the weapons used by the Babylonians to carry on their military conquests.

God also uses the catching of fish as a figure of speech, but He catches fish to save them, not to destroy them. You remember that the Lord Jesus said to some of His own disciples who were fishermen, "You have been catching fish and that's fine, but I am going to give you a job of catching *men*" (see Matt. 4:19). My friend, to me the greatest business in the world is to be a fisherman, and that is all I claim to be. We are to fish for men in our day.

"Therefore they sacrifice unto their net, and burn incense unto their drag." The Babylonians were pagans, of course, and gave no credit to the true and living God for their successes.

There are fishermen here in Southern California who think that they get a good catch because their priest has blessed the fishing fleet.

That has nothing in the world to do with it, my friend. The reason that you can get plenty to eat is that God is *good*, and that is the only reason. God is good, and He is the one who provides.

Shall they therefore empty their net, and not spare continually to slay the nations? [Hab. 1:17].

Habakkuk is asking God, "Are You going to permit them to go on into the future, destroying people after people?" God's answer is, "No, I'm going to send Judah into captivity in Babylon as a chastisement, a judgment for her sins, but then I will judge Babylon." My friend, God did exactly that, and in our day Babylon lies under the dust and rubble of the ages. It is a silent but eloquent testimony that God does judge evil.

Now let's translate this interrogation of Habakkuk into the times in which we live. Why does God permit evil? Well, He permits it because He is long-suffering. He is not willing that any should perish, and He has provided a cross, a crucified Savior, so that no one needs to perish. This He did at the first coming of Christ.

Habakkuk's second question is, "Why does not God judge the wicked?" God will answer that at the second coming of Christ, because at that time He will judge sin. All we need is a perspective to see the answers to these two questions. Christ came the first time to wear a crown of thorns and to die upon a cross. The next time He comes, He will wear a crown of glory and will hold the scepter that will rule the earth.

To make a personal application of this, we ask the question, "Why does God permit this trial to happen to me?" I do not know what the answer is for you, but God has an answer.

Several years ago I stayed in a motel in Siloam Springs, Arkansas, at a location where I could throw a rock into the state of Oklahoma. My dad is buried over there. When I was a boy of fourteen, I stood by his grave and wept. He had been killed in an accident at a cotton gin. After the funeral service was over and everyone had gone, I rode back on my bicycle to his grave. I wept and cried, "Why, oh God, did You take him?" Time has gone by, and today I have an answer for that. I know now that it was God's method of dealing with a boy who would never have entered the ministry otherwise.

Actually, what right do we have to question our Maker? What right does little man have to look into the face of heaven and demand, "Why do you do this?" Well, to begin with, it is none of our business. It is God's business. This is His universe, and He is running it to please Himself. We are to trust Him.

I can remember when I was a little boy in Oklahoma, we lived in an area that had many tornadoes. In the night my dad would pick me up, and I would begin to cry and ask, "Where are we going?" He would take me down to the storm cellar where it was dark and damp and not very comfortable. He would put me on a pallet, and in the morning I would awaken and be safe and secure. When I was a crying little boy, my dad didn't explain tornadoes to me. He simply protected me from them. All I knew was that I trusted my dad. After my dad died, I learned more and more to trust my Heavenly Father. There are times He has done things to me that He hasn't explained. He took my first child, and I really had a question about that. Do you want to know something? I still have a question mark about it. But I do know this: He has the answer. Someday He will tell me the answer. In the meantime, I'll trust Him.

CHAPTER 2

THEME: The perception of the prophet

In chapter 1 we saw the perplexity of the prophet. Now the prophet has learned that God has answers for his questions. He answered his first question, which raised a bigger question, but God has an answer for that also.

My friend, if you have a question, don't smother it in pious phraseology. I often hear people say, "Oh, I'm trusting the Lord, " when they are not trusting Him; they are questioning Him every step of the way. There is no sin in questioning the Lord. Just go to Him and tell Him that you don't understand. This is what Habakkuk did.

PRACTICE OF THE PROPHET

I will stand upon my watch, and set me upon the tower, and will watch to see what he will say unto me, and what I shall answer when I am reproved [Hab. 2:1].

Habakkuk says that he is going to the watchtower to wait. (When he says, "watchtower," he doesn't mean that he is going to read a magazine!) Prophets are compared to watchmen in several of the books of prophecy. For instance, in Ezekiel it was, "Son of man, I have made thee a watchman unto the house of Israel: therefore hear the word at my mouth, and give them warning from me" (Ezek. 3:17). The prophets were watchmen who were to prophesy to the nation, and God would hold them responsible for giving out His warning. In a walled city the watchman was the one who watched for enemies during the night; if he was faithful, the city was safe. But if he should betray the city or fail to sound the alarm when an enemy approached, the city was in deep trouble. So Habakkuk, God's prophet, says that he is going to the watchtower to wait for a message from God.

"I . . . will watch to see what he will say unto me." Habakkuk is saying, "I'm going to wait patiently, because I know that God has an answer. I don't know what it will be, but I know He has an answer and He will give that answer in due time."

"And what I shall answer when I am reproved." The word reprove here is not the best translation of the original word: Habakkuk did not expect God to rebuke him or, to use the common colloquialism, "bawl him out" because he was questioning God's ways. Habakkuk felt that God would give him the right answer so he would understand God's ways. And he was willing to wait for it.

God often delays. He moves slowly in all that He does. God intends to give Habakkuk an answer, but it will come in His own time. We are the ones who are in a hurry; God is not. For example, sometimes we hear Christians speak of the "soon coming of Christ." Can you show me in the Bible where that is found? I have never found it. Jesus said, "Behold, I come quickly . . ." (Rev. 22:7, italics mine). He didn't say He was coming soon. It has now been over nineteen hundred years since He spoke those words, and that could hardly be called soon. He said He would return quickly, because the things that are mentioned in Revelation, which will happen just before He returns to earth, are going to happen quickly. The thing which will introduce the last seven years before Christ comes to establish His Kingdom will be the rapture of the church. When the church leaves the earth, events will move quickly—like a trip-hammer, one blow right after another. Christ will come quickly. He will come right on schedule. We are not to look for the soon coming of Christ but the imminent coming of Christ.

Neither will Christ "delay" His coming, as I hear some pious brothers say. The Lord is coming on His schedule—nor mine nor yours. He will not delay. But we must remember that the Lord is long-suffering. He is patient. He is not willing that any should perish. And in Habakkuk's day there was a company of people down yonder in Babylon whom God was going to save. That seventy-year captivity of the children of Israel was going to be a glorious time for God because He was going to reach even the heart of Nebuchadnezzar, king of the Babylonians!

Habakkuk says, "I'm going to retire now to my watchtower. I don't have the answer, but I'm going to wait for an answer from God." And, my friend, you and I are to walk by faith and not by sight. In 2 Corinthians 5 the apostle Paul speaks of the time when our bodies will be put into the grave. The day will come when Christ will call us and raise up our bodies from the grave. In the meantime, when we are absent from the body, we are present with the Lord. When we leave these bodies, we are going to be at home with the Lord. There is an interval of time between the burial of our bodies and the resurrection of our bodies. The Lord moves slowly as judged by the way we look at things. That is why Paul interposes here, "For we walk by faith, not by sight:" (2 Cor. 5:7). Do you have questions which have not been answered? I do. But I have learned, as I did as a little boy when my dad picked me up and carried me to the storm cellar, that my Heavenly Father also has reasons for the things He does in my life. Although I don't always understand them now, I know that He has the answer, and someday He will give it to me. We need to trust Him.

PATIENCE OF THE PROPHET

And the Lord answered me, and said, Write the vision, and make it plain upon tables, that he may run that readeth it [Hab. 2:2]

God is saying, "Write it so that those folk in the twentieth century—especially that fellow, McGee, who will have some questions [and I think He had you in mind also]—will have an answer from Me during the days when they will be walking by faith."

"That he may run that readeth it." We sometimes get that turned around and make it say, "That he who runs may read it." That is not what God is saying. He says that we need to have a road map with us. We need to know where we are going. We need to know a great deal about the way so that, after we have read it, we may run. That is, the one reading it was to run to tell it forth; he was to be the messenger of God's Word.

My friend, there are many folk today who are trying to preach and trying to teach God's Word without adequate preparation. They need to do more reading before they start running. I remember when I wanted to enter into the ministry, I thought I would skip part of my college training and bypass seminary and go immediately to a Bible school and then start preaching. I thank God for a marvelous, wonderful pastor who told me to get all the training I could get. Learn to read before you start running. Before you begin to witness, be able to give a reason for the hope that is in you.

> **For the vision is yet for an appointed time, but at the end it shall speak, and not lie: though it tarry, wait for it; because it will surely come, it will not tarry [Hab. 2:3].**

"For the vision is yet for an appointed time, but at the end it shall speak." There is no better way to explain this than to quote a note on this verse in *The New Scofield Reference Bible* (p. 954):

> To the watching prophet comes the response of the vision (vv. 2–20). Three elements are to be distinguished: (1) The moral judgment of the LORD upon the evil practiced by Israel (vv. 5–13, 15–19). (2) The future purpose of God that "the earth shall be filled with the knowledge of the glory of the LORD, as the waters cover the sea" (v. 14). That this revelation awaits the return of the Lord in glory is shown (a) by the parallel passage in Isa. 11:9–12; and (b) by the quotation of v. 3 in Heb. 10:37–38, where the "it" of the vision becomes "he" and refers to the return of the Lord. It is then, after the vision is fulfilled, that "the knowledge of the glory," etc. shall fill the earth. But (3) meantime, "the just shall live by his faith." This great evangelical word is applied to Jews and Gentiles in Rom. 1:17; to the Gentiles in Gal. 3:11–14; and to the Hebrews especially in Heb. 10:38. This opening of life to faith alone, makes possible not only the salvation of the Gentiles, but also makes possible a believing remnant in Israel while the nation, as such, is in blindness and unbelief (see Rom. 11:1 and 5, *notes*), with neither priesthood nor temple, and consequently unable to keep the ordinances of the law. Such is the LORD! In disciplinary gov-

ernment His ancient Israel is cast out of the land and judicially
blinded (2 Cor. 3:12–15), but in covenanted mercy the individual Jew may resort to the simple faith of Abraham (Gen. 15:6;
Rom. 4:1–5) and be saved. This, however, does not set aside the
Palestinian and Davidic Covenants (see Dt. 30:3 and 2 Sam.
7:16, notes), for "the earth shall be filled," etc. (v. 14), and the
Lord will again be in His Temple (v. 20). Cp. Rom. 11:25–27.

My friend, you can depend on the fact that someday God will give us
the answers to all of our questions. That is going to be a great day! I am
not interested in heaven's golden streets, but I am very interested in
learning the answers to a great many questions that puzzle mankind
in our day. In the meantime, we are to walk by faith.

PAGEANT FOR THE PROPHET

This brings us to one of the most important verses in the Scriptures.
It is the key to the little Book of Habakkuk. And, actually, it gives the
key to the three great doctrinal epistles in the New Testament that
quote this verse: Romans 1:17; Galatians 3:11; and Hebrews 10:38.

**Behold, his soul which is lifted up is not upright in him:
but the just shall live by his faith [Hab. 2:4].**

"The just shall live by his faith." There have been many ways of attempting to sidestep the tremendous impact of this verse. Some have
attempted to interpret "faith" as faithfulness or right dealing—the
just shall live by his faithfulness. However, this verse gives us the two
ways which are opened up to mankind.

Notice that the verse mentions two groups of individuals which
are in the world: (1) the lifted-up or puffed-up souls; and (2) the just
man who is living by his faith. In other words, you could call them the
lost and the saved, those who have trusted God and those who have
not believed God. Or you can call them the saints and the ain'ts—that
makes a sharp division also.

You remember that verse 1 told us that Habakkuk has gone to his watchtower to wait for the answer of God. It will be God's great message which will explain His dealings with individuals and with nations. So here in verse 4 we have a great principle that God has laid down. Actually, it is an axiom of the Bible.

You will remember that when you studied geometry, you accepted certain axioms which were self-evident and you didn't have to prove. For example, a straight line is the shortest distance between two points. And there are certain statements in the Scriptures which are great axioms. This is one of them: "Behold, his soul which is lifted up is not upright in him."

"His soul which is lifted up is not upright in him" describes a group of people who are proud. Either they are attempting to work out their own salvation, or they are just living for today with the philosophy of "eat, drink, and be merry for tomorrow we die." They have no real goal in life. "His soul . . . is not upright in him." He is wrong. He is going down the wrong pathway. "There is a way which seemeth right unto a man, but the end thereof are the ways of death" (Prov. 14:12). You know, I am sure, many folk in this group of humanity. They have a lifted-up or puffed-up soul. They are lifted up with pride. As they meander along their way, picking daisies as they go, they move as on a slow-moving river and will finally arrive at the sea of destruction. That is their end. The Scriptures seldom enlarge upon the fate of the lost, but our Lord Jesus followed them through when He told of the rich man and Lazarus (see Luke 16). When Lazarus died, he was carried to paradise; when the rich man died, he went to hades. He went, as it was said of Judas, to his own place. If you go through life like this, your end will be the same.

"The just shall live by his faith" describes the second group of the human family. They are flowing down the river of life toward the city of God and toward full knowledge—". . . then shall I know even as also I am known" (1 Cor. 13:12, italics mine). Between the moment of salvation and the *then*, the saved ones will walk by faith. We may not have the answers to our questions now, but God will give them to us when we arrive in His presence.

Now because Habakkuk 2:4 is quoted in the New Testament and is actually the key to the Epistles of Romans, Galatians, and Hebrews, let's look at these quotations more carefully.

In the Epistle to the Romans, the emphasis is upon justification by faith for salvation. "For I am not ashamed of the gospel of Christ: for it is the power of God unto salvation to every one that believeth; to the Jew first, and also to the Greek. For therein is the righteousness of God revealed from faith to faith: as it is written, *The just shall live by faith*" (Rom. 1:16–17, italics mine). The point here is that "the just," the one who has been justified by faith, shall also live by faith. And that is the great message of the Epistle to the Romans.

In the Epistle to the Galatians, the quotation is this: "But that no man is justified by the law in the sight of God, it is evident: for, *The just shall live by faith*" (Gal. 3:11, italics mine). The emphasis is a little different here, for we find in Galatians 2:20, "I am crucified with Christ: nevertheless I live; yet not I, but Christ liveth in me: and the life which I now live in the flesh I live by the faith of the Son of God, who loved me, and gave himself for me." While in Romans the emphasis was on justification by faith for salvation, in Galatians the emphasis is not only on faith that saves, but on a faith by which you live throughout life.

In the Epistle to the Hebrews, the quotation from Habakkuk 2:4 is this: "Now the just shall live by faith: but if any man draw back, my soul shall have no pleasure in him" (Heb. 10:38). Here the emphasis is upon the word *live*—"the just shall *live* by faith." And in the following chapter, we read of men and women who lived by faith—the emphasis is upon *living*.

When Habakkuk looked into the future, he asked, 'Why, God?" Now from our vantage point, we can look back into history and see the answer to Habakkuk's question. God sent His own people into captivity because it served the purpose of chastisement for their sins. And now we see His greater purpose: it enabled Him to bring the Savior into the world—in the fullness of time.

Again I want to draw your attention to Paul's great sermon at Antioch of Pisidia: "But he, whom God raised again, saw no corruption. Be it known unto you therefore, men and brethren, that through this man is preached unto you the forgiveness of sins: and by him all that believe are justified from all things, from which ye could not be justified by the law of Moses. Beware therefore, lest that come upon you, which is spoken of in the prophets; behold, ye despisers, and wonder, and perish: for I work a work in your days, a work which ye shall in no wise believe, though a man declare it unto you" (Acts 13:37–41). Therefore, Paul shuts them in to only one way to God—faith. The message is: ". . . Christ died for our sins according to the scriptures; and that he was buried, and that he rose again the third day according to the scriptures" (1 Cor. 15:3–4).

And what are we to do? We are to accept Him as our Savior. We are to trust Him and walk by faith—not by law. I am disturbed when I see so many folk today who are attempting to put believers back under the Ten Commandments or under some little legal system that they have worked out, such as rules and regulations for the family—for the husband and for the wife and for the child. Oh, my friend, if you have been saved by faith in the Lord Jesus Christ, *love Him.* Loving Him will work out your problems. Loving Him will enable you to walk in the Spirit; and walking in the Spirit, you will be filled with the Spirit, and you will have joy in your heart. You will be a better husband or a better wife or a better child. You will be a better employee or a better employer. Wherever you are, you will be a better person if you walk by faith, and one of these days you will walk right into His presence and be with Him throughout eternity.

Habakkuk was a man of faith. He said, "I'll go to my watchtower and wait for God's answer. I am trusting the One who does have the answer." You see, ". . . without faith it is impossible to please him; for he that cometh to God must believe that he is, and that he is a rewarder of them that diligently seek him" (Heb. 11:6). And the "just shall *live* by his faith." My friend, today God is asking you to come to Him, and the only way you can come to Him is by faith. The man of faith receives life by faith, he walks by faith, and he moves into eternity by faith—not by his own ability but on the strength and the ability of Another.

Let me repeat that Habakkuk 2:4 gives the two ways which are opened up to mankind. Our Lord Jesus put it like this: "Enter ye in at the strait gate: for wide is the gate, and broad is the way, that leadeth to destruction, and many there be which go in thereat: because strait is the gate, and narrow is the way, which leadeth unto life, and few there be that find it" (Matt. 7:13–14).

The broad way is actually like a funnel. It is very wide at the place where you enter, but it narrows down so that the follower ends up in only one place—destruction. That is the story of the unbelieving sinner. It is like going down a canyon. I have experienced this when I have been hunting out here in the West. You can start out in the desert in a very wide, open spot. Soon you enter into a canyon; and, as you go deeper and deeper into the canyon, the floor of the canyon gets narrower and narrower. That is the picture here. The entrance is wide, but the end narrows down to destruction.

The straight gate, or the narrow gate, is also an entrance into a funnel. In this case, the gate or entrance is very narrow. Jesus Christ said, ". . . I am the way, the truth, and the life: no man cometh unto the Father, but by me" (John 14:6). That entrance is narrowed down to one person. He is the way. He doesn't just show us the way; He *is* the way. "He that hath the Son hath life; and he that hath not the Son of God hath not life" (1 John 5:12). You either have Christ, or you don't have Him. You either trust Him, or you don't trust Him. Your salvation has nothing in the world to do with going through a ceremony or making pledges or going forward in a meeting or in joining a church. Your salvation is dependent upon your relationship with Jesus Christ. That is the reason it is a narrow gate. God has given to the world just this one way. The issue is what you will do with Jesus Christ who died on the Cross and rose again. That is why Jesus said, ". . . strait is the gate, and narrow is the way, which leadeth unto life, and few there be that find it" (Matt. 7:14).

This gate is also like a funnel. You enter in at the narrow gate— Christ is the way. But as you enter, it doesn't narrow down even more. No, it widens out. Jesus said, ". . . I am come that they might have life, and that they might have it more abundantly" (John 10:10). Oh, the freedom and liberty He gives to those who are His own!

Let me give an example. Alcohol addiction and drug addition can look like a broad road of liberty, but they end in the narrow canyon of destruction. My dad used to say, "I can drink, or I can let it alone." He died when I was fourteen. He was a heavy drinker, but he was never an alcoholic. When I was a boy, I would talk to him about his heavy drinking and ask why he didn't give it up. He would say, "Son, I can give it up any time I want to." Do you know what his problem was? He didn't want to. Had he lived longer, I am confident the day would have come when he would have found himself in a very narrow canyon with only one alternative, and that would be to take another drink.

Now the Christian who went in the narrow gate by trusting Christ as his Savior never gets to the place where it narrows down. He really is *living*. If you really want to live, come to Christ.

PARABLE TO THE PROPHET

Now how about the other crowd—those whose soul "is not upright in him"? The following "woes" are directed to them and refer primarily to the plundering Babylonians who would conquer Judah. These "woes" are just about as systematic and orderly as anything you will find in Scripture. They are presented in five stanzas of three verses each.

Yea also, because he transgresseth by wine, he is a proud man, neither keepeth at home, who enlargeth his desire as hell, and is as death, and cannot be satisfied, but gathereth unto him all nations, and heapeth unto him all people [Hab. 2:5].

"Yea also, because he transgresseth by wine." He is talking about the Babylonians. At that moment Babylon was not the great nation that it became later at the time of Daniel.

The first charge is that they transgressed by wine and were proud. "Neither keepeth at home"—they longed to go forth and conquer. "But gathereth unto him all nations, and heapeth unto him all people." They were inflamed with an ambition for conquest. They were never satisfied but kept attacking nation after nation, gathering spoil and captives. Babylon became the first great world power. They wanted to rule the world. That has been the ambition of a great many nations of the world. I am afraid that after World War II the United States got that insane notion also. We stuck our nose into the affairs of other countries when we should have kept our nose at home where it belonged. This has been the fallacy of the nations of the world, and it was the fallacy of Babylon. They were lifted up with pride and felt they were capable of ruling the world.

Notice that God mentions their sin of drunkenness. This issue comes up several times in the writings of the prophets: in Amos, Joel, Nahum, and now Habakkuk. Nahum makes it clear that drunkenness brought down the kingdom of Assyria. Amos tells us that it was drunkenness that caused God to send the northern kingdom into captivity. Now Habakkuk says that it is drunkenness that will cause God to destroy Babylon. In other words, drunkenness works out its own destruction. Drunkenness characterized Babylon. Read Daniel 5, which tells of Belshazzar's great feast. That was the night that Babylon fell. Why? They were drunk! It was a night of revelry and drunkenness. They felt perfectly safe and secure in their fortified city.

Drunkenness brought down Rome also. On our tour to Bible lands, I have taken groups of people to a place many of them had never heard of. It is Ostia, about fifteen miles from Rome, down by the Tiber River on the seacoast. The ruins at Ostia reveal that there the Romans gave themselves over to revelry and drunkenness—those were the things that brought them there. It was the playground of the Romans.

And drunkenness will destroy our own nation. As I travel across this country, I stay in many of the hotels, motels, and inns where conventions are in progress. As I have observed them, they are times of great revelry and drinking. Recently in Dallas, Texas, there were two conventions going on at one time while we were there. On the way to the service in the evening, we would pass two big rooms where cocktail parties were in progress. Now these were the conventions of two reputable companies in this country, but that was the way they carried on their business. How long will a nation last that has millions of alcoholics?

Here in the little Book of Habakkuk, God says that drunkenness has led to pride and has made you like "hell" or sheol—you want to gobble up everything. The Book of Proverbs puts it this way: "The horseleach hath two daughters, crying, give, give. There are three things that are never satisfied, yea, four things say not, It is enough: The grave . . ." (Prov. 30:15–16). The grave is sheol, and it is first on the list. Habakkuk uses the same expression, "who enlargeth his desire as hell [sheol]"—continuing to expand their borders, moving out, never, never satisfied.

Now God spells out the five woes upon Babylon.

> **Shall not all these take up a parable against him, and a taunting proverb against him, and say, Woe to him that increaseth that which is not his! how long? and to him that ladeth himself with thick clay! [Hab. 2:6].**

The first woe is a taunting proverb against Babylon because they were seizing by force that which was not theirs.

"Shall not all these take up a parable against him." The "all these" probably refers to the nations that have been victims of Babylon's aggression.

"To him that ladeth himself with thick clay!" A better translation is "and maketh himself rich with loans," which makes more sense. It is one thing to buy property and pay for it, but it is another thing to take it by force. God is pronouncing a woe against this nation for wanting more and taking that which does not belong to them.

You see, God has planned that man by the sweat of his brow is going to make his living. And, my friend, if you are not earning your living by the sweat of your brow, somebody else is doing it for you. Babylon wanted somebody else to do the work, and then they by force would take it away. That is the first woe—God is going to judge Babylon for that, and He is just and righteous for doing it.

> **Shall they not rise up suddenly that shall bite thee, and awake that shall vex thee, and thou shalt be for booties unto them? [Hab. 2:7].**

"And thou shalt be for booties unto them?" is the principle that whatever a man sows, that shall he also reap. God is saying, "You take it away from somebody, then somebody else will take it away from you." The fact is that when Media-Persia became a great nation, they took Babylon. By night the River Euphrates, which flowed through the city of Babylon, was cut off and the water diverted into other channels, leaving a dry riverbed through the city. And Gobryas, the Median general, marched his army along that riverbed into the city and took it by surprise.

> **Because thou hast spoiled many nations, all the remnant of the people shall spoil thee; because of men's blood, and for the violence of the land, of the city, and of all that dwell therein [Hab. 2:8].**

Man is bloodthirsty, and man is coveteous.

The second woe is for their covetousness and their self-aggrandizement—

> **Woe to him that coveteth an evil covetousness to his house, that he may set his nest on high, that he may be delivered from the power of evil!**

> **Thou hast consulted shame to thy house by cutting off many people, and hast sinned against thy soul.**

> **For the stone shall cry out of the wall, and the beam out of the timber shall answer it [Hab. 2:9–11].**

Covetousness was a sin of Babylon along with drunkenness. Their covetousness was an evil kind of coveting. They wanted that which did not belong to them. God tells us we are not to covet our neighbor's property or our neighbor's wife or our neighbor's wealth.

"That he may set his nest on high, that he may be delivered from the power of evil!" This is likening Babylon to an eagle who feels that his nest is absolutely impregnable.

"Thou hast consulted shame to thy house . . . and hast sinned against thy soul." Babylon brought the judgment of God itself by its covetousness and bloodshed. Even the stones would cry out against them. Contrast this to the time in the life of the Lord Jesus when the religious rulers tried to silence the crowd who were singing hosannas to Him. He said, ". . . I tell you that, if these should hold their peace, the stones would immediately cry out" (Luke 19:40).

The third woe has to do with murder and pillage, slaughter and violence—

> **Woe to him that buildeth a town with blood, and stablisheth a city by iniquity! [Hab. 2:12].**

This was the method of destruction that built Babylon. They became rich by warfare.

My friend, if you stand back and look at the history of mankind, you come to the conclusion that he must be insane the way that he has lived on this earth. And, actually, he is insane—insane with a sinful nature so that he can't even direct his path. He thinks he is right in what he does. People have never waged war without thinking they were doing the right thing. We see here God's condemnation of Babylon, but it can be stretched out and brought up to date and fitted like a glove on any modern nation you choose.

> **Behold, is it not of the LORD of hosts that the people shall labour in the very fire, and the people shall weary themselves for very vanity? [Hab. 2:13].**

This verse could be translated: "Behold, is it not of the LORD of hosts that the peoples shall labor only for fire, and the nations shall weary themselves for nothing?" Think of the futile efforts that have been made by the great nations of the past. Instead of building up, they have spent more time in tearing down. Look at Greece, for instance, and their marvelous, wonderful pieces of architecture, the statues, the art, and literature; but actually, the Greeks spent more time in destruction. If you follow the march of Alexander the Great as he crossed over into Asia, you will notice that he did nothing in the world but destroy one city after another, one great civilization after another. That was the thing that marked him out. And that is the thing that marked out Babylon, the nation about which Habakkuk is prophesying.

> **For the earth shall be filled with the knowledge of the glory of the Lord, as the waters cover the sea [Hab. 2:14].**

This is the far-off goal toward which God is moving. This will be fulfilled when the Lord Jesus Christ returns to the earth (see Isa. 11:9).

> **Woe unto him that giveth his neighbour drink, that puttest thy bottle to him, and makest him drunken also, that thou mayest look on their nakedness! [Hab. 2:15].**

This is actually a little different from the drunkenness mentioned in verse 5. There God says, "He transgresseth by wine." Here He says, "Woe unto him that giveth his neighbour drink, that puttest thy bottle to him, and makes him drunken also, that thou mayest look on their nakedness!" The tragic thing is that liquor is something that leads to gross immorality. It leads to the breaking down of morals. It leads men to commit sins they otherwise probably would not commit—dishonesty and many other sins.

Drunkenness is an alarming problem in many of our large corporations today. I have talked with a man here in Southern California who holds a very responsible position in a large corporation and with another man who is connected with one of the big banks in our state. They both tell me that their corporations have employed certain officials whose business it is to watch for any of their men who are beginning to drink too much. They have many ways of discerning this. They will talk to his wife and have him followed at night if certain things begin to show in his work—if he is late to work or perhaps doesn't even show up for work. Because some of these men are brilliant men, good men, the company officials will go to them, confront them with their drinking problem, and offer to help them to give it up. But notice how crazy this is: on one hand, these companies have cocktail parties where their men get drunk, and on the other hand, they have a process for drying them out! That is sort of like running a hospital where you bring in healthy people, give them disease germs, and then treat them for the disease they get! Man becomes sort of a guinea pig in this crazy world in which we live today. So many illogical things are being done even by large corporations.

This is the condemnation that is here brought against Babylon. God says to them, "You are making drunkards. Not only are you drinking yourselves, but you are also making drunkards of others."

Again may I refer to an authority, a man and his wife who are working with young people who are caught up in the drug culture. They tell me that many of these young people have come out of homes where cocktails are served. If Mama and Papa are going to have cocktails and live their lives, why can't Junior have his drugs? I would like to have a good answer for that because Junior has asked that question of me. I don't have an answer for him because I think Mama and Papa are responsible for his going into this drug culture. I believe that behind the problem of drugs has been drunkenness. Drunkenness is the thing that has brought this to pass in our nation today.

I know that these things are not being said today, and I know that it does not make me very popular to say them. But I don't think Habakkuk was too popular himself—certainly not down in Babylon when this word percolated down there. But they found out that God condemns drunkenness and that God condemns making drunkards of others.

Notice that drunkenness leads to gross immorality—

> **Thou art filled with share for glory: drink thou also, and let thy foreskin be uncovered: the cup of the LORD's right hand shall be turned unto thee, and shameful spewing shall be on thy glory [Hab. 2:16].**

Drunkenness leads to gross immorality. It leads to divorce. It leads to the breaking up of homes. It leads to a life of sin. I have come to the place in my own life that I have lost respect for men in government. These fellows talk so big about honesty, and they talk so big and brave

about helping the poor, while it is a well-known fact that many of
them are actually alcoholics who drink like fish. May I ask you, how
can we have respect for government when this sort of thing is all out
in the open? Yet they ask us to respect them, to look up to them, and to
give them our support. It makes me bow my head in shame to see
what is happening in this great land of ours. My friend, Habakkuk
spelled it out here years ago. God says, "The reason I will bring Babylon down is because of these sins."

> **For the violence of Lebanon shall cover thee, and the
> spoil of beasts, which made them afraid, because of
> men's blood, and for the violence of the land, of the city,
> and of all that dwell therein [Hab. 2:17].**

Violence is another of the fruits which comes from drunkenness. You
see, all kinds of immoralities spring from drunkenness. The drug culture, the gross immorality, the prevalence of divorce—all of these sins
that are abroad in our land today—have come out of drunkenness.

The fifth woe is God's condemnation of the greatest sin of all—

> **What profiteth the graven image that the maker thereof
> hath graven it; the molten image, and a teacher of lies,
> that the maker of his work trusteth therein, to make
> dumb idols?**

> **Woe unto him that saith to the wood, Awake; to the
> dumb stone, Arise, it shall teach! Behold, it is laid over
> with gold and silver, and there is no breath at all in the
> midst of it [Hab. 2:18–19].**

Actually, drunkenness is not the greatest sin. The greatest sin is idolatry, false religion, turning to an idol instead of turning to God. This is
the worst sin of all.

In the Book of Judges a great principle of government is presented,
a principle which is also stated very clearly in the prophecy of Isaiah.
All of the subsequent prophets simply bear out and apply this princi-

ple which has already been stated. The principle is this: There are three steps in the downfall of a nation. First of all, there is *religious apostasy.* The second step is *moral awfulness.* And the third step is *political anarchy.* These are the three steps by which nations pass off the stage of human history. That has always been the way it has moved. You see, the primary problem never was political anarchy. The primary problem never was moral awfulness. As bad as these are, the root problem goes back to religious or spiritual apostasy, a turning away from the living and true God.

This is the thing which has happened to my nation today, and I am not the only one who is saying this, by any means. A prominent professor of history has made the statement that the American dream is vanishing in the midst of terrifying realities and visible signs of decadence in our contemporary society. Clinton Rossiter, at one time a professor of American history at Cornell University, said that in our youth we had a profound sense of national purpose that we lost over the years of our rise to glory. James Reston of the *New York Times* (and I don't think anybody has ever called him a conservative) has said that in public they talk about how optimistic and wonderful the future is, but that the private conversations of thoughtful men in Washington are quite different. It is his opinion that for the first time since World War II, one begins to hear of doubts that mortal man is capable of solving or even controlling the political, social, and economic problems that life has placed before him. This is the picture and this is the story of the downfall of nations, and it alarms me. This great principle, which this man Habakkuk has again restated in the Word of God, was fulfilled in the nation of Babylon.

The downfall of a nation begins in idolatry; it begins in turning away from the living and true God. We would like to think that idolatry has gone out of style, that no one today in this country is bowing down to an idol. That, of course, is not true. Many a man today is worshiping the almighty dollar. Many a man worships sex. Many a man worships pleasure. Many a woman has given her virtue in order to become a famous star or in order to be promoted. May I say to you, anything that you give yourself to, anything that takes all your time or energy, anything that takes all of you is what you worship. That, my friend, is your god, that is your idol, and that is what God condemns. God says that He is a jealous God. God says, "I made you. I created you. I have redeemed you. And I want you." When a man turns his back on God, he is doing the worst thing any man can possibly do.

> **But the Lord is in his holy temple: let all the earth keep silence before him [Hab. 2:20].**

Personally, I believe this looks to the future when the Lord Jesus Christ will come to the earth. When He is in His temple down here, the whole earth will be silent before Him. All of the noise, all of the clamor, all of the protest, all of the confusion will disappear at that time. But it is also true that it applies to today. The reason we are having all these difficulties and problems down here is that, although He is yonder in heaven, although the Lord is in His temple, man does not bow before Him and recognize Him. It would be a wonderful thing if we could just have a week of silence. Wouldn't it be wonderful if everyone in Washington, D.C., would keep his mouth shut for a week? Wouldn't it be wonderful if all of us preachers on radio would keep our mouths shut? Wouldn't it be a wonderful thing if everyone who is doing so much talking would just keep quiet and wait before almighty God?

"The Lord is in his holy temple: let all the earth keep silence before him." But the second psalm opens with a question mark—Why? Just like Habakkuk's questions, the psalmist asks, "Why do the heathen rage, and the people imagine a vain thing?" (Ps. 2:1). Why all the clamor? Why all the protest? Because they are far from God. The nations have forgotten that God today is in His heaven. Browning was wrong when he said that God is in His heaven and all's right with the world. God is in His heaven, but all is *wrong* with the world because man is not rightly related to God. Our problem today is a problem of man's relationship to God. My friend, there is only one alternative, there is only one way out: "The just shall live by his faith" (v. 4).

CHAPTER 3

THEME: The pleasure of the prophet

As we come to the third chapter of Habakkuk, a tremendous change has taken place in the life of this man Habakkuk. When we get to the end of this chapter, we will see that this man has made a right about-face. The book opened in gloom—Habakkuk has a question mark for a brain, and he has questioned God. But now it closes in glory with a great exclamation point. It closes on a high note of praise, and you will not find any more confident faith than that which is expressed in the last part of this book.

We can divide this chapter into three very definite sections. In the first two verses, we have the prayer of the prophet. We have the program of God in verses 3–17, and then we have the position of the prophet in verses 18–19.

PRAYER OF THE PROPHET

A prayer of Habakkuk the prophet upon Shigionoth [Hab. 3:1].

Shigionoth is a word having to do with music. Some think it might have been some sort of a musical point used to indicate to the musician the way the piece was to be played. Others think it was a musical instrument. We also find this word in the Book of Psalms (the singular form, *shiggaion*, is used in the title to Psalm 7). We know it has to do with music, and Habakkuk's prayer is Hebrew poetry. It is a song of high praise.

What a change has taken place in the life of Habakkuk! His glorious experience on the watchtower and his patient waiting for an answer from God have brought him into a place of real faith and have opened his eyes to something he was not conscious of before. Therefore, this chapter is his song. I would call it a folk song; it's a happy song. It is to be played with a stringed instrument, according to the last sentence of this chapter, which says, "To the chief singer on my stringed instruments" (v. 19). I suppose that this is a little notation which Habakkuk put there to indicate how this song was to be sung. Perhaps he is telling the soloist to get with it, that this was something to be sung with a stringed instrument. Aren't most of the folk songs today sung with a stringed instrument? You and I may not like these stringed instruments and what is coming from them, but nevertheless, stringed instruments are used for folk singing. Apparently, that is what we have here in this chapter, but it was on a much higher plane than the music I hear today.

I do not choose to listen to our modern music, but I often have to hear it. It is amazing that we hear so much about freedom of speech, but what about freedom of hearing? I'd like to have my ears protected today. Just because some vile person insists upon his freedom of speech, my ears are offended because I have to listen to singing that I don't care for. I am forced to hear at least a segment of a dirty song—in my judgment, it is a dirty song—but he's got to have *his* liberty. We today don't consider that we ought to have a little freedom of our ears and not have to listen to a lot of the junk that is being passed around.

> **O LORD, I have heard thy speech, and was afraid: O LORD, revive thy work in the midst of the years, in the midst of the years make known; in wrath remember mercy [Hab. 3:2].**

Habakkuk's song is a wonderful song. I do not think this would be offensive to anyone's ears. It is a beautiful prayer. Habakkuk says, "O LORD, I have heard thy speech." In other words, God has answered him. God has said to him, "Now look here, Habakkuk. I want you to stay in your watchtower, and I want you to walk by faith. I want you to trust Me. You think that I am not doing anything about the sins of My people, but I am. I am preparing a nation, the Chaldeans, or the Babylonians, and they are going to be used as I used the Assyrians against the northern kingdom of Israel—they were the 'rod of my anger.' But when I am through with the Babylonians, I am going to judge them, and I will judge them on a righteous basis." God's judgment of Babylon was spelled out in chapter 2 in the five woes, the great national sins which brought that nation down. God was moving to bring Babylon down.

The very interesting thing is that Habakkuk now reverses himself. He says, "I've heard Your speech, and I am afraid." What is he afraid of? Well, he had thought that God wasn't doing anything. Now he is afraid the Lord is doing too much!

Notice what Habakkuk says: "O LORD, revive thy work in the midst of the years, in the midst of the years make known; in wrath remember mercy." He says, "Lord, I didn't think You were working. I didn't think that You were doing anything, but I see now that You are moving in judgment. And since You are moving in judgment, remember to be merciful even to the Chaldeans, and be merciful to Your people." Before, Habakkuk had been calling down fire from heaven not only upon his own nation who had departed from God but also upon the Chaldeans. Now he is saying, "Lord, don't forget to be merciful." Well, God is merciful, and God is gracious. He is not willing that any should perish.

It does look today as if God is not doing anything, but if you and I could ascend to the watchtower of Habakkuk, if we could learn that the just shall live by his faith, if we could have a living faith in God and see what is moving behind the scenes and see the wheels that are turning, I think that we would be as surprised as this man was. I am not sure but that we, too, would cry out to God for mercy. A great many Christians today have thrown up their hands about the conditions in our own country—they've just given up. We all feel that way at times, don't we? But, may I say to you, God *is* moving today in judgment, and somebody needs to cry out to Him and say, "Oh, Lord, in wrath, as You are moving in judgment, don't forget to be merciful to us. We need Your mercy." This great nation of ours needs the mercy of God today. Since World War II, we have been on an ego trip. We have really had a flight of pride, of being the greatest nation in the world, and now even our little gas buggies have been slowed down.

We feel almost helpless today. What would we do in the time of a major crisis? Suppose we were attacked from the outside, how much gasoline would there be? How much of the many other chemicals that are so needed would there be? How long would we really last? It is my belief that God is moving in judgment, and we need to ask Him to be merciful to us. Shakespeare has Portia say in *The Merchant of Venice* (Act IV, Scene i):

> The quality of mercy is not strain'd
> It droppeth as the gentle rain from heaven
> Upon the place beneath: it is twice blest.

We need His mercy. We talk about showers of blessing—what we need today are showers of mercy from almighty God.

What a reversal has taken place in the thinking of this man Habakkuk. At first he said, "You are not doing anything, Lord. Why don't You do something? Why do You let them get by with their sin?" Now God has let Habakkuk see that He is doing something, and Habakkuk cries out for the mercy of God. If we really knew how much God is moving in judgment, I am of the opinion that it would bring America to her knees before Almighty God.

Let us move on down into this very wonderful prayer. Habakkuk's prayer is actually a recital of what God has done in the past history of the people of Israel. In view of the fact that He has done it in the past, He intends to do it again in the future—that is the thought here. You can depend upon God's continuing to do what He has done in the past. Paul wrote about this to us as believers—in fact, this is my life verse: "Being confident of this very thing, that he which hath begun a good work in you will perform it until the day of Jesus Christ" (Phil. 1:6). My friend, has God begun a good work in you? He has brought you up to this present moment, has He not? He has begun a good work in you, and you can be sure He will perform it until the day of Jesus Christ, until He takes you out of this world and you will be in His likeness. This is our confidence, and this is the great confidence of this psalm of Habakkuk.

PROGRAM OF GOD

In this section I believe there are three men in the background. However, none of them is mentioned by name, because this is not a psalm about what any man has done; it is a psalm about what God has done through men. Therefore, the men are not mentioned by name. Many scholars see only two men here. But I believe that we have Abraham (vv. 3–6), Moses (vv. 7–10), and Joshua (vv. 11–15). However, there are many who feel that Moses is the only one mentioned in verses 3–10.

> **God came from Teman, and the Holy One from mount Paran. Selah. His glory covered the heavens, and the earth was full of his praise [Hab. 3:3].**

Teman is in Edom, and Paran is nearby in the Sinaitic Peninsula. Many think this is a reference to the time when the children of Israel came up out of the land of Egypt. However, you will recall that Abraham went down to Egypt even before that time.

Selah is a very interesting word which is also found in the Psalms. Its use here would indicate again that this is a psalm. There is a difference of viewpoint as to what selah means. Some believe that it marks a pause in the music, a breathing place. Some think it means that this is where the drums should come in and the music reach a high crescendo. Well, I'm not very musical—in fact, I am not musical at all. To me, I think of it as meaning, "Stop, look, and listen." At all the railroad crossings when I was a boy a cross was put up which said, "Stop, Look, and Listen." That is what I think selah means. God is saying, "Now sit up and take notice. Be sure to hear this." The singer is to really let go and the drummer to really pound the drums at this point. Selah is to call attention to what has been said. Whether this verse speaks of Abraham or Moses is unimportant because God was present with both of these men.

We have a marvelous, wonderful picture here of the glory of God: "His glory covered the heavens, and the earth was full of his praise." Well, that hasn't taken place quite yet. But certainly, as far as Abraham was concerned, there was praise in his heart. And for the children of Israel when they came out of Egypt, at first at least, there was praise in their hearts. Of course, they became complainers and whiners during the rest of the journey.

"His glory covered the heavens." We need to be impressed today as believers with the glory of our God. How majestic, how powerful, how wonderful is our God!

> **And his brightness was as the light; he had horns coming out of his hand: and there was the hiding of his power [Hab. 3:4].**

"And his brightness was as the light; he had horns coming out of his hand." These "horns" are spokes of light, rays of light. As you know, when the sun comes up, rays of light shoot up from it. This is the picture we are given of His approach. I think that when the Lord Jesus comes back to take His church out of this world, a glory will be present that was not present when He was born in Bethlehem. That will also be true when He comes to the earth to establish His Kingdom.

"And there was the hiding of his power." In other words, the glory of God so covered Him that you could not see Him. The very glory of God obscures the glory of God, if you please. Oh, the majesty of His person! This is something which believers need to recognize and respect.

> **Before him went the pestilence, and burning coals went forth at his feet [Hab. 3:5].**

This could apply to the time of Moses in Egypt and the ten plagues; but it also could apply to Abraham who went down to Egypt because there was a famine, a pestilence, in the land.

> **He stood, and measured the earth: he beheld, and drove asunder the nations; and the everlasting mountains**

were scattered, the perpetual hills did bow: his ways are everlasting [Hab. 3:6].

"He stood, and measured the earth." Remember that God said to Abraham, "I am going to give you this land," and He measured it out to him. God has made the statement that He has lined up the nations of the world according to the way He gave that land to Abraham. That is an amazing thing, by the way.

"He beheld, and drove asunder the nations; and the everlasting mountains were scattered, the perpetual hills did bow: his ways are everlasting." Oh, the ways of our God are past finding out! This is a marvelous psalm, my friend.

I saw the tents of Cushan in affliction: and the curtains of the land of Midian did tremble [Hab. 3:7].

"I saw the tents of Cushan in affliction"—Cushan is Ethiopia. "And the curtains of the land of Midian did tremble." You will recall that this man Moses went down into the land of Midian for a time. It is believed now by some scholars that Moses, as the son of Pharaoh's daughter, probably led a campaign into Ethiopia. That, of course, is not really a matter of record but rather the belief of some scholars. We do know that he ". . . was mighty in words and in deeds" (Acts 7:22).

Was the LORD displeased against the rivers? was thine anger against the rivers? was thy wrath against the sea, that thou didst ride upon thine horses and thy chariots of salvation? [Hab. 3:8].

This is a reference to the children of Israel crossing the Red Sea and crossing the Jordan River. God opened up the waters for them. This is highly figurative, beautiful language, by the way. It is Hebrew poetry, and it speaks of the fact that God was not angry with the rivers because they blocked the way; rather, He merely opened up the Red Sea and let the people cross over, as He did again later with the Jordan River.

Thy bow was made quite naked, according to the oaths of the tribes, even thy word. Selah. Thou didst cleave the earth with rivers [Hab. 3:9].

"Thy bow was made quite naked, according to the oaths of the tribes, even thy word. Selah." God was making good His covenant, His promise, to His people. Believe me, "selah" means that you need to pound those drums again, drummer. This should wake them up and cause them to listen to what God has to say.

"Thou didst cleave the earth with rivers." Have you ever stopped to think how God has sliced this earth with rivers? The rivers are like great slices down through the earth. What a highly figurative but accurate picture is given to us here!

The mountains saw thee, and they trembled: the overflowing of the water passed by: the deep uttered his voice, and lifted up his hands on high [Hab. 3:10].

When Moses went up to receive the Law on top of Mount Sinai, the mountain trembled, and the children of Israel were so frightened that they actually did not want to come near it. They didn't want God to speak to them at all—they were absolutely frightened.

These verses are a picture of how God through Moses delivered the children of Israel. First, God made a covenant with Abraham, and He made it good. Then God made a covenant with Moses that He would deliver the children of Israel out of the land of Egypt. He made that covenant good also, and He delivered them as He had said He would.

In verse 11 we come to Joshua. I think it is quite clear that Joshua is in the background here but, as I said before, the names of these men are not mentioned because the emphasis is upon the acts of God.

The sun and moon stood still in their habitation: at the light of thine arrows they went, and at the shining of thy glittering spear [Hab. 3:11].

"The sun and moon stood still in their habitation"—this immediately identifies this with Joshua.

"At the light of thine arrows they went, and at the shining of thy glittering spear." In other words, the very shining of the sun was like a glittering spear.

> **Thou didst march through the land in indignation, thou didst thresh the heathen in anger [Hab. 3:12].**

When God put His people in that land, He put them in there and removed the Amorites because of the sin in their lives. The Amorites who occupied the section in which Jericho was located were eaten up with venereal disease. God moved them out of that land because they would have infected the entire human family. It was almost a plague among them in those days.

> **Thou wentest forth for the salvation of thy people, even for salvation with thine anointed; thou woundedst the head out of the house of the wicked, by discovering the foundation unto the neck. Selah [Hab. 3:13].**

There has been a question as to whether "then anointed" refers to Israel or to the Messiah. Personally, I think it means the Messiah here. "Thou wentest forth for the salvation of thy people, even for salvation with thine anointed"—it is the Lord Jesus who is the Savior as well as the Anointed One, the Messiah.

"Thou woundedst the head out of the house of the wicked, by discovering the foundation unto the neck. Selah." When the "anointed one" is mentioned here, the music is to reach the highest crescendo, what is called fortissimo. Here is where you need a good soprano and a good basso. This is great praise unto God for the salvation which He wrought for these people. He delivered them out of Egypt under Moses, and He brought them into the land through Joshua, but these were all the acts of God.

> **Thou didst strike through with his staves the head of his villages: they came out as a whirlwind to scatter me: their rejoicing was as to devour the poor secretly.**

> **Thou didst walk through the sea with thine horses, through the heap of great waters [Hab. 3:14–15].**

This was God making good His promises, and this was His salvation to them.

We come now to the reaction of the prophet to all of this. I could only wish that I could do justice to the remainder of this little book and of this chapter. I know that I am totally inadequate to present it as it should be presented to you. This is one of the great passages of the Word of God. I wish that somehow I could convey to your heart something of the grandeur and the glory that is here.

> **When I heard, my belly trembled; my lips quivered at the voice: rottenness entered into my bones, and I trembled in myself, that I might rest in the day of trouble: when he cometh up unto the people, he will invade them with his troops [Hab. 3:16].**

At the end of this book, Habakkuk now gives us his own personal experience. He opened the book, as we have seen, with his own personal experience. He tells now about his own physical reaction to all of this. Did you ever have that sinking feeling in the pit of your tummy when some crisis faced you or you came to some place in life where there was a great emergency? This was Habakkuk's experience. He says, "When I heard, my belly trembled; my lips quivered at the voice." Have you ever been so frightened that you could not speak audibly? I am sure that most of us have had an experience like that.

I had that kind of an experience as a young man when I was going to see a certain young lady. The girl who lived next door to her also had a young man who was keeping company with her. After this other young man and I would leave their homes in the evening, there apparently was a Peeping Tom who had found a place on the porch where he could look into both of their bedrooms at the same time. Each of these girls had a sister, so that there were two girls in each home. Apparently, he had been doing this for some time. One evening, the girls next door thought they saw him pass by their window, and so they called to the home where I was. Very foolishly, the girl brought me her father's pistol, and I walked to the alley in the back where there was a high fence. I was walking back to the house, getting ready to tell the girls there wasn't anybody back there. All of a sudden, a form appeared right above me on that fence. That fellow could have jumped down upon me, but he was so frightened at seeing me that he didn't budge—and neither did I! I tried to raise the gun to shoot, and I thank God I was so frightened that I was not able to do it. I tried to talk, but I couldn't say anything. The girl called her father and said, "He's choking Vernon out there!" He wasn't choking me—I was so scared I just couldn't open my mouth. Instead of being a hero like I intended to be that evening, I turned out to be a very sorry one. That fellow, whoever he was, dropped down on the other side of the fence and started running. I set the gun on the fence because I couldn't hold it steady, and I shot at him twice, but he was perfectly safe. I don't think my shots got in his neighborhood at all! I remember that experience as a time when I felt what Habakkuk describes, but mine was only a chance encounter.

Habakkuk says, "Rottenness entered into my bones." That means he couldn't stand up—he had to hold on to something. "And I trembled in myself, that I might rest in the day of trouble." He saw that God was going to move in judgment, and he knew that it was going to be a hard and difficult time.

Although the fig tree shall not blossom, neither shall fruit be in the vines; the labour of the olive shall fail, and the fields shall yield no meat; the flock shall be cut off from the fold, and there shall be no herd in the stalls [Hab. 3:17].

Habakkuk says, "There will be no fruit on the trees, there will be no grapes, the livestock will be gone." All of this will be a part of the judgment of God.

POSITION OF THE PROPHET

In spite of the impending judgment, Habakkuk is able to say—

> Yet I will rejoice in the LORD, I will joy in the God of my salvation.
>
> The LORD God is my strength, and he will make my feet like hinds' feet, and he will make me to walk upon mine high places. To the chief singer on my stringed instruments [Hab. 3:18–19].

I want you to understand that God is our strength and our joy. God has not promised peace and prosperity in these days in which we live. So much is being promised to us today! I just threw into the wastebasket a magazine which comes from a so-called Christian organization and which told about all the things that you can get through prayer. The magazine promised that God will make you prosperous, that He will give you health, and that He will give you everything. My friend, God is not a glorified Santa Claus! But our God is moving in a very definite way. If you want an answer to your problems, Habakkuk gives you the answer here. That answer is simply this: God is the answer to your problems.

In the beginning of this book, Habakkuk came to God and said, "Why are You doing these things? Why are You permitting me to see evil? Why don't You move?" God brought Habakkuk to the watchtower and let him see what He was doing, and now Habakkuk says, "I am going to walk by faith with God." My friend, God is the answer to your problem today. I don't know who you are or what your problem is, but God is the answer. You can have faith and confidence in Him. God has a purpose in your life, and He intends to carry it through. You can trust Christ, and, when you trust Him, you will find that He begins to work in you. He wants to conform you to His image—it is God's intention to make you like Christ.

The apostle Paul writes: "And we know that all things work together for good to them that love God, to them who are the called according to his purpose. For whom he did foreknow, he also did predestinate to be conformed to the image of his Son, that he might be the firstborn among many brethren" (Rom. 8:28–29). Regardless of the big words Paul uses, he simply means that God's eternal purpose with you is to make you like Jesus Christ. Again, he writes in 2 Corinthians: "But we all, with open face beholding as in a glass the glory of the Lord, are changed into the same image from glory to glory, even as by the Spirit of the Lord" (2 Cor. 3:18). My friend, God has a purpose for you. It does not matter who you are. To say that someone else has a greater purpose in life than you have is entirely wrong. You are as important in God's plan and purpose as any individual who has ever lived on this earth or who ever will live on this earth. He wants to make you like Christ. We read in 1 Corinthians 15:47–49: "The first man is of the earth, earthy: the second man is the Lord from heaven. As is the earthy, such are they also that are earthy: and as is the heavenly, such are they also that are heavenly. And as we have borne the image of the earthy, we shall also bear the image of the heavenly." We are down here in these human bodies which have actually been taken out of the dirt; and God has made us human beings, but that is not His final purpose. We are earthy, but He wants us to be heavenly, and that is His goal for us.

Imagine that you live in the day of Michelangelo. One day you visit his studio, and you see there a rough piece of stone, which is dirty and polluted because it has come out of a dark and damp quarry. It is a hard piece of marble—crude, unyielding, cold, unlovely, and unsightly. But you come back in six months, and what has happened? Why, it has become a statue of David or of the archangel Michael. May I say to you, just as Michelangelo had a purpose for that crude piece of marble, God has a purpose for you and me today. We are earthy, but He has a heavenly purpose for us. You see, the ideal of the artist (who is the Holy Spirit) is to conform us to the image of Christ. The chisel He uses is the discipline of the Lord—"For whom the Lord loveth he chasteneth . . ." (Heb. 12:6). And the hammer is the Word of God. And therefore we can say with the psalmist, ". . . I shall be satisfied, when I awake, with thy likeness" (Ps. 17:15).

My friend, God is the answer to your questions. God is the answer to your problems. Therefore, it does not matter who you are or where you are; you can rejoice in Him, and you can rejoice in His salvation. You can say with Habakkuk, who was such a pessimist in the beginning, "I will joy in the God of my salvation." This book opened in gloom, but it closes in glory. It opened with a question mark, but it closes with a mighty exclamation point. And it ends with his wonderful song. May you and I be encouraged today by the Word of God!

BIBLIOGRAPHY

(Recommended for Further Study)

Feinberg, Charles L. *The Minor Prophets*. Chicago, Illinois: Moody Press, 1976.

Freeman, Hobart E. *Nahum, Zephaniah, and Habakkuk*. Chicago, Illinois: Moody Press, 1973.

Gaebelein, Arno C. *The Annotated Bible*. 1917. Reprint. Neptune, New Jersey: Loizeaux Brothers, 1971.

Ironside, H. A. *The Minor Prophets*. Neptune, New Jersey: Loizeaux Brothers, n.d.

Jensen, Irving L. *Minor Prophets of Judah*. Chicago, Illinois: Moody Press, 1975. (Obadiah, Joel, Micah, Nahum, Zephaniah, and Habakkuk.)

Tatford, Frederick A. *The Minor Prophets*. Minneapolis, Minnesota: Klock & Klock, n.d.

Unger, Merrill F. *Unger's Commentary on the Old Testament*, Vol. 2. Chicago, Illinois: Moody Press, 1982.